# People Management Practice:

## *A handbook for practices*

Vasthiyampillai Sivalogathasan

# People Management Practice:

# A handbook for practices

By

Vasthiyampilai Sivalogathasan

First Edition 2011

ISBN:10-1461050839
ISBN-13:978-1461050834

Printed by CreateSpace,
a DBA of on-Demand Publishing LLC,
part of the Amazon group of companies,
www.CreateSpace.com
www.Amazon.com

7290 B, Investment Drive
Charleston, SC 29418, USA .
PR@CreateSpace.com

# DEDICATION

To my parents and my teachers who have given me the light of knowledge and support throughout my life. And also to my wife and children who have always stood by me and dealt with all of my absence with a smile.

# CONTENTS

# ACKNOWLEDGMENTS

This book has been published with support of the CreateSpace during my PhD study in the Zhejiang University, Hangzhou, China. I would like to thank Vice-Chancellor of the Open University of Sri Lanka, Dean of Faculty of Humanities and Social Science, Head of Department of Management Studies and all members of Department of Management Studies. I am grateful to the very many individuals and organizations who have shared their thoughts and experiences on earlier my Assignments. Especially thanks to Professor. Xiaobo Wu who is my supervisor for PhD study in the field of Innovation Management at Zhejiang University, China. And also thanks to the Chinese Scholarship Council who granted full scholarship for my PhD Studies. Any errors or misunderstandings are my own acknowledgments.

# PREFACE

Excellence people management practice depend on getting the right people in the right place at the right time and keeping them there. It is also difficult for an organization to achieve purpose, clarity and consistency in effective people management practice without some expert support from a trained HR professional.

People management might be defined as having the strategic people management practices in place to promote employee engagement. Employee engagement is the extent to which people in an organization are passionate about what they do and the lengths they will go to in order to achieve their own performance objectives and the wider organizational goals.

Positive people management practice lead to greater staff satisfaction and employee engagement, which in turn lead to a higher probability of high performance. Management practice should be specified in clear leadership competencies and people management objectives against which line managers should be assessed rigorously.

HR can drive strategy and support managers those at the top and in line management roles, to ensure that they are skilled and competent in the key areas of people management. Many surveys confirm that employees function better and feel more comfortable where there are clear and transparent expectations, ways of working and policies and procedures. However, you can only turn this clarity into credibility if all of these are applied consistently. Therefore, we look beyond theory with pragmatic guidance about putting the principles into practice.

**V.Sivalogathasan.**
B.Com(Hons); MBA(IB).
MIPM(SL); MIM(SL); SLAAS; HRP.
PhD Scholar,
Zhejiang University, China.
December 2011

# 1  INTRODUCTION TO PEOPLE  MANAGEMENT

## 1.1.  People Management Practice

People are the assets on which competitive advantage is built, whether in the public or private sector, whether in the corporate world or in the world of education. In the words of the latest theory on human resource management, people are an "inimitable" asset. The one thing that competitor organizations cannot imitate is people and their skills. So human resource management and the practices associated with it have become accepted by managers in all forms of organizations as one of the most important strategic levers to ensure continuing success (Boxall and Purcell, 2003).

This includes all the individual employees who contribute to the operation of an organization. Whether they are employed full time, part time, temporary or permanent basis. The concept of human resources include the energies, skills, talent and knowledge of people which are, or which potentially can be applied to the production of goods or the rendering of useful services. When they manage people they need to remember that these particular resources are special, and are ultimately the most important assets. People are the only real source of 'core competence' (Prahalad and Hamel, 1990) and thus of continuing competitive advantage.

The definition of terms such as 'personnel management' and 'human resource management' is one area of particular confusion and irritation to general managers, and we will discuss later the differences between what typically is meant by these terms. We will use the phrase 'people management' as a generic term to cover both 'personnel management' (PM) and 'human resource management' (HRM) in the absence of a

1

specific definition of either.

But broadly, we can say that the 'people management' function – whether we wish to define it as 'personnel management' or as 'human resource management' – may be described as:

All the management decisions and actions that directly affect or influence people as members of the organization rather than as job-holders.

In other words, people management is not executive management of individuals and their jobs. Management of specific tasks and responsibilities is the concern of the employee's immediate supervisor or manager – that is, the person to whom his or her performance is accountable (sometimes this might be the person's team). So people managers – whether 'personnel managers' or 'human resource managers' – do not have line authority over employees.

The term 'human resource management' was being used by Peter Ducker and others in North America as early as the 1950s without any special meaning, and usually simply as another label for 'personnel management' or 'personnel administration'. By the 1980s, however, HRM had come to mean a 'radically different philosophy and approach to the management of people at work' (Storey, 1989) with an emphasis on performance, workers' commitment and rewards based on individual or team contribution, differing significantly in all of these from the corresponding aspects of traditional personnel management .

One of the main characteristics of HRM is the devolution of many aspects of 'people management' from specialists directly to line managers. HRM itself has been called 'the discovery of personnel management by chief executives'. So line managers over the past ten years or so have frequently been confronted with HRM decisions and activities in their day-to-day business in a way that was not the case previously.

This process has been accelerated by a more recent development which adds to the burden of the line manager while increasing the effectiveness of the organization as a whole. Outsourcing of large areas of the traditional personnel management department's routine functions is happening on a massive scale. This is unlikely to be a passing fad. Outsourcing of non-core functions, allowing the organization to concentrate on its core competencies, has been one of the single most important organizational factors in both business and the public sector in recent years. It is extremely unlikely that this will be set in reverse in the foreseeable future.

A common definition of HRM is that it encompasses the philosophies, policies and practices that affect the employee working for the organization (Hellriegel et al. 1999). This is a very broad definition includes activities related to hiring, education and training, performance review, compensation etc., HRM refers to practices of people management that aim to enhance organizational performance by improving the performance of individuals within the organization, they include practices such as recruitment, selection, induction, training, performance appraisal and design and application of reward systems. HRM also refers to the strategies developed by organizations for people management and their alignment to broader organizational strategies.

HR is "the total inherent knowledge, abilities and skills that the workforce processes as a whole and the beliefs, attitudes and values they have individually" It is not merely the number of heads in the organization. That is why the capacity of HR doesn't depend on its number of employees. Therefore "managing a workforce to achieve organizational objectives while achieving their own objectives" is known as HRM. Hence attraction of HR, development of HR and maintaining and retaining of HR for organizational excellence can be defined as HRM.

Michael Armstrong (1996) has conceptualized HRM as "A strategic and coherent approach to the management of an organization's most valued assets the people working there who individually and collectively contribute to the achievement of the objectives of the business".

### Importance of People Management Practices

Today, the importance of the people in the organization is increasing their competencies, talents, intellectuality, abilities and personalities. The world is changing so fast that the forces the changes are sometimes beyond the capacity of people. The managers have to depend on their HR to be better able to respond to change people in organizations are considered to be assets that have value and likely to generate income for the organization not just hand and minds that are hired for a wage or salary. There are some of the forms of change and the influence of these such as. Workforce diversity, Technology, Globalization, Legal Issues, The nature of work, Mergers and acquisitions, Organizational Structure, Increased competition, Increased ethical and social responsibility.

### 1.1.1. Evolution and Gradual Development of HRM practices

The concept of HRM is fairly a recent development. It is basically a different attitude to words the people in organization personnel management has been a recent phenomenon, the discipline and subject have been evident over several centuries in history, the evidence has taken the form if certain practice and procedures that have been followed by individuals and communities.

*The ancient times:* The earliest evidence of HRM practices known to mankind were those relating to personnel decisions taken in primitive societies. These societies developed and practiced certain mechanisms notably, in the selection process of tribal leaders. In addition, there is evidence of decision relating to training of youth in primitive activities such as hunting, preparation and cooking of food they had also developed knowledge to protect the safety and health of the group.

*The Industrial Revolution:* The prevalent method of manufacture of staple commodities from the 16th century through to the early part of 18th century was the cottage system. Merchants typically paid individuals for work performed in their cottages to produce goods from raw materials provided by them. Eventually, however, the cottage system gave way to the factory system this was known as the industrial revolution. The industrial revolution began in England. However it was not until about 1860 that mass production Technology flourished in the United Status. In spite of the increased wealth that the industrial revolution generated, the factory system had many shortcomings that were detrimental to its workers.

*The Labour Unions Present:* American labour union have existed and presented for improved wages and working condition since the 1740s the earliest national federation of Unions still existing today is the American Federation of labour, founded in 1886. The Wagner Act is the basic labour law in the United States today, which was established in 1935. It gave unions much more power in dealing with management and made labour a much more formidable match for personnel managers. Overall, there has been a better treatment of employees.

## 1.1.2. Personnel Management and Human Resource Management

Organized personnel work in industry appears to have emerged around about the 1900s. The first fully-fledged "employment department" appeared at that time at the B.F. Good rich company.

The emergence of personnel management has been attributed to two diverse fields of Endeavour. There are the industrial welfare movement and scientific management. The industrial welfare movement, derived from religion and etc., led some organizations to set such as libraries, financial assistance for education, recreational facilities and medical care.

The emergence of modern personnel administration was scientific management that Fredrick W. Taylor developed. Taylor's basic objective was to develop more efficient way of performing work at the lowest level in industrialized organizations among workers at the shop level.

Important milestone in the Personnel Management and HRM to People Management
✓ World War I created a labour shortage which made turnover a calamity and tardiness and absenteeism serious problems and the

organizations (1910)"discovered" that labour turnover as a costly proposition many organizations developed personnel departments to deal with these problems.

✓ Many business firms tried to be 'good' to their employees on the assumption that their workers would consequently be more satisfied and work harder. Significant research at Western Electric company's Hawthorne plant (1920) indicated that interpersonal relationships and group behaviour were indeed important in organizations.

✓ The Wagner Act and the Social Security Act 1935 are special importance in this period as part of the social security Act, unemployment compensation a cooperative federal state piece of legislation was passed and still operating today. As such, this stage (1930s) was referred to as the "personnel administration" stage.

✓ The spotlight on personnel management was intensified during world war II. End of world war II, (1940) the personnel department has continued to grow it has been faced with increasingly expanding and complex technology. Among such technological changes, computerization and automation stand out as probably the most important to the personnel manager.

✓ The extensive social legislation passed since the 1960s have affected personnel management for example: in the United States. The equal pay Act. of 1963, had been designed to equalize the pay of men and women doing equal jobs. The massive civil rights Act. Of 1964, aimed at protecting individuals from discrimination on the basis of race, color, sex, national origin and religion. The occupational safety at health act of 1970s was geared to improving safety and health conditions.

✓ In 1980, to be characteristic of human resource management phase one personnel management become more and more management and business oriented. The personnel manager was expected to be a business partner at this stage. Strategic HRM also become prominent at this stage.

✓ The emergence of team work, improvement and continuous improvement and organizations were considered to be learning organizations in 1990. Quality becomes the way of life of managers.

✓ A growing emphasis on knowledge workers and human capital. Human capital refers to the knowledge, education, training, skills, and expertise of a firm's workers. Today the center of gravity in employment is moving fast from manual and clerical workers to knowledge workers. In this environment managers need new world class HR management systems and skills to select, train, and motivate employees and to get them work more like committed partners. People Management Practice to be innovative and creative for firm innovation and competitive advantage.

Personnel management characteristically focused on a range of activities centered on the supply and development of labour to meet the immediate and short-term organizational needs. Under personal management the activities of recruitment, selection, rewards development and others are viewed as separate individual functions. HRM aims to integrate all of the personnel function into a cohesive strategy. Personnel management was largely something that managers did to subordinates, whereas HRM takes the entire organization as a focal point for analysis and stresses development at all levels (Legge, 1995).

## 1.2. Functions and Operations in HRM

When we look at more specifically, we can suggest that it is a process consisting of four functions.
1. Acquisition – getting people
2. Development – preparing them
3. Motivation-activating them
4. Maintenance-keeping them.

## Acquisition Function

It begins with planning, this includes the estimating of demands and supplies of labour acquisition also include the recruitment, selection, hiring and socialization of employees.

To face constant change which emerges due to the uncertainty is not an easy task. This necessitates proper HR planning which consists of the identification of the types of jobs needed along with their job requirements.

Staffing refers to HR planning, recruiting, selecting, orienting, promoting and termination processes. Promotions and terminations also are increasingly important in today's HRM issues. Like other HRM decisions, staffing decisions also have legal ramifications. Companies are very conscious about legal aspects when making staffing decisions.

### Development Function

It includes employees training, performance management, development and carrier development. Organizations constantly develop and take measures to improve their Human Resources. Technology is always changing and this demands that the employees should have the capacity to fit into there new requirements and procedures. Now ideas regarding organizational productivity are constantly immerging. Due to the present legal set up in the country organizations should provide some measures and improve accordingly.

### Motivation Function

It includes job satisfaction, performance appraisal, behaviour and structural techniques, for stimulating worker performance the importance of linking rewards to performance compensation.

Organizations compensate employees through wages and salaries, bonuses, and benefits such as health insurance, vacation time, and pension programs. These activities are very important in achieving HRM goals. The person requires more encouragement through promotions skill development through training etc.

### Maintenance Function

In contrast to the motivation function which attempts to stimulate performance, the maintenance function is concerned with providing these making conditions that employees believe are necessary in order to maintain their commitment to the organization.

### 1.2.1 Line Manager's HRM Responsibilities

The direct handling of people is, and always has been, an integral part of every line manager's responsibility, from president down to the lowest level supervisor. For example, one major company outlines its line supervisor's responsibilities for effective human resource management under the following general headings.
1. Placing the right person on right job.

2. Starting new employees in the organization (orientation)
3. Training employees for jobs that are new to them.
4. Improving the job performance of each person
5. Gaining creative cooperation and developing smooth working relationships
6. Interpreting the company's policies and procedures
7. Controlling labour costs
8. Developing the abilities of each person
9. Creating and maintaining departmental morale
10. Protecting employee's health and physical condition

In small organizations, line managers may carry out all these personnel duties unassisted. But as the organization grows, they need the assistance, specialized knowledge, and advice of a separate human resource staff.

## 1.2.2 Responsibilities of the Human Resource Manager

Although line managers and HR managers need to work together, their responsibilities are different. The major activities for which an HR manager is typically responsible are as follows:

*Advice and counsel*: The HR manager often serves as an in-house consultant to supervisors, managers, and executives. Given their knowledge of internal employment issues. (Policies, labour agreements, past practices, and the needs of employees) as well as their awareness of external trends (economic and deployment data, legal issues, and the like), HR managers can be an invaluable resource for making decisions.

*Service:* HR managers also engage in a host of service activities such as recruiting, selecting, testing, planning, and conducting training programmes, and hearing employee concerns and complaints. Technical expertise in these areas is essential for HR managers and forms the basis of HR program design and implementation.

*Policy formulation and implementation*: HR managers generally propose and draft new policies or policy revisions to cover recurring problems or to prevent anticipated problems. Ordinarily, these are proposed to the senior executives of the organization, who actually issues the policies. HR managers may monitor performance of line departments and other staff departments to ensure conformity with established HR policies, procedures, and practice.

*Employee advocacy:* One of the enduring roles of HR managers are to service as an employee advocate listening to the employees concerns and representing their needs to managers. Effective changes interfere with normal daily activities.

### 1.2.3 Legal aspects of HRM

As every day passes, there is new legislation is all parts of the world. A manager has to be responsible to comply with these regulations in an ethical manner. For example, there are laws pertaining to equal opportunities for employment with the intention than an individual's gender, ethnicity, religion and such other personal characteristics will not Linder that person's recruitment to an organization. Health and occupational safety measures, health incentives, collective bargaining are now mandated. Thus managers have deal with the issues relating to these laws in the workplace with the assistance of HR managers.

Maintaining effective relationship between employer and employee gives two benefits basically, first; employees who are dissatisfied are most likely to quit. Poor employee – employer relationships can create many problems for the organization. Secondly there are several laws pertaining to the employer-employee relationship.

Every time you advertise a job opening, or recruit, interview, test, or select a candidate or appraise an employee, you have to take equal employment laws into account.

An unlawful employment practice is established when the complaining party demonstrates that race, color, religion, sex or national origin was a motivating factor for any employment practice, even though other factors also motivated the practice.

### 1.3. Strategic Human Resource Management

Human resources play in an organization's success or failure and its ability to respond to the numerous challenges that emerge. The strand of thinking has led to HRM being conceptualized as Strategic Human Resource Management.

Truss and Gratton (1994) have defined Strategic HRM as
".......the linking of HRM with strategic goals and objectives in order to improve business performance and develop organizational cultures that foster innovation and flexibility.......".

Armstrong, M (1996) has suggested that
Strategic HRM can be regarded as an approach to dealing with longer-term people issues as part of the strategic management trust of the business. It covers macro-organizational concerns relating to structure and culture, organizational effectiveness and performance, matching resources to failure business requirements, and the management of change.

SHRM is for all employees in all levels of the organization. Therefore Human Resource Managers take the 'strategic' perspective in the HR function addressing some of the challenges they face in enhancing competitive advantage, core competencies, critical success factors and synergy.

## 1.3.1 Environmental Factors affecting HRM activities

Categories of environmental factors are twofold namely Internal and External. Internal factors are those that emerge within the organization and these factors such as work structure and business strategy are unbreakable. External Factors emerge from outside the company.

### *External Environment*

As from outside of company, these factors including business conditions. Workforce characteristics, laws, unions and technology are beyond the organizations control. For example, globalization of business is an external aspect which affects the organization.

Unions also have a major effect on HRM practices. For example, most unionized organizations base HRM decisions more on seniority than organizations that are not unionized.

Finally, technology also has a major effect on HRM practices. The production facility of yesterday, for instance relied more on the sheer 'physical stamina and strength of is workforce than on the highly automated production facility of today; which relied more on mental abilities and teamwork.

### *Internal Environment*

Moving out from traditional organizational structure has created many implications to the HRM activities today. By elimination of hierarchy of the structure, promotion opportunities are also eliminated. This affects the motivation of employees.

Organization's business strategy also has major implications for HRM activities. Some companies emphasize on customer services where as some companies emphasize on price of the product. All their decisions regarding price and handling of customers depend on their objectives.

## 1.3.2 Dimensions of Strategic Human Resource Management

I.      *Re engineering the business process*

This is fairly a new concept which is practiced in many of the present successful organizations. We should know that reengineering of business process means the fundamental rethinking and radical redesign of business process to achieve dramatic improvements in critical, contemporary measures of performances, such as cost, quality, service and speed. (Hammer and Champy – 1993 ) under this process every possible effort is taken to upgrade the quality and enhance the productivity of the products of the company.

## II.    Leadership
This concept of leadership is also available in SHRM.  Leadership reflects the assumption that leadership involves a process whereby an individual exerts influence upon others in an organizational context. In a strategic HR environment, leadership is more complex and we can explain it as the process where an individual member of a group or organization influences the interpretation of events, the choice of objectives and strategies, the organization of work activities, the motivation of people to achieve the objectives, the maintenance of co-operative relationships, the development of skills and confidence by members and the enlistment of support and co-operation from people outside the group or organization.

## III.    Workplace learning
It is an interdisciplinary body of knowledge and theoretical inquiry that draws upon adult learning and management theory.  In practice, it is that part of the management process that attempts to facilitate work related continuous learning at the individual, group or organizational level.  In strategic HRM, it is needed to establish this type of culture and environment in the organization.

## IV. Trade Unions
If all workers are fully integrated into the business they will identify with their company goals and management problems, so that what is good for the company and management & perceived by workers as also being good for them.  Trade unions are an instrument that unites all the employees of an organization into cohesive group. Therefore to be strategic, HR should maintain a positive and healthy relationship between unions.

## V. Organizational Performance
Through SHRM, organizations are more likely to achieve high performance. Organizational performance comprises the actual output or results of an organization as measured against its intended outputs (or goals and objectives).

According to Richard et al. (2009) organizational performance encompasses three specific areas of firm outcomes: (a) financial performance (profits, return on assets, return on investment, etc.); (b) product market performance (sales, market share, etc.); and (c) shareholder return (total shareholder return, economic value added, etc.).[1] The term Organizational effectiveness is broader. Specialists in many fields are concerned with organizational performance including strategic planners, operations, finance, legal, and organizational development. Integrating strategy, HRM and organizational outcomes should help to guide and contribute to more effective use of and decisions about, human resource.

### 1.3.3 Competitive Advantage through People

Global rivalry, shorter product life cycles, and unstable product and market environments have contributed to a new business world that offers some interesting challenges and opportunities to organizations. Established competitive mechanisms have become less useful response, and therefore firms continuously seek for newer sources of competitive advantage, one of the most important being human resource management (HRM) (Jayaram et alL.,1999; Terpstra, 1994). Survival and success of organizations increasingly depend on their ability to build highly skilled work forces and to release the full potential of their human resources.

While people have always been central to organizations, today they have taken on an even more central role in building a firm's competitive advantage. Particularly in knowledge-based industries such as software and information services, success increasingly depends on "people-embodied know-how," the knowledge, skills and abilities imbedded in an organization's members. In fact, a growing number of experts now argue that the key to a firm's success is based on establishing a set of core competencies-intergraded knowledge sets within an organization that distinguish it from its competitors and deliver value to customers.

Organizations can achieve sustained competitive advantage through people those who are able to meet the following criteria.

1.  The resources must be of value. People are a source of competitive advantage when they improve the efficiency or effectiveness of the company. Value is increased when employees find ways to decrease costs, provide something unique to customers, or some combination of the two.
2.  The resources must be rare. People are a source of competitive advantage when their skills, knowledge, and abilities are not equally available to competitors.
3.  The resource must be difficult to imitate. People are a source of competitive advantage when employee capabilities and contribution cannot be copied by others.

4.    The resource must be organized. People are source of competitive advantage when their talents can be combined and deployed to work on new assignments at a moment's notice.

## 1.3.4 Competitive Challenge and Human Resource Management

For over a decade, there have been a variety of important developments in the literature concerning the issues pertaining to the management of people and significant attention has been directed towards HRM practices (Haris and Ogbonna, 2001). HR practitioners have become busy with indicating the value of the HRM, mostly through showing its impact on firm performance, the society for human resource management and the commerce clearing house have sponsored and ongoing study of the most important competitive trends and issues facing HR.  These key trends extend beyond "people issues", but they all focus on the need to develop a skilled and flexible work force in order to compete in the twenty-first century:

• Going global
• Embracing new technology
• Managing change
• Developing Human Capital
• Responding to the market
• Implementation of SHRM

*Going Global*
In order to grow and prosper, many companies are seeking business opportunities in global markets.  Competition and cooperation with foreign companies have become increasingly important focal point for business since the early 1980s. For all the opportunities afforded by international business, when managers talk about "going global", they have to balance a complicated set of issues related to different geographies, culture, laws, and business practices.

*Embracing New Technology*
Advancements in computer technology have enabled organizations to take advantage of the information explosion. Which computer networks, unlimited amounts of data can be stored, retrieved, and used in a wide variety of ways, from simple record keeping to controlling complex equipment.  Information Technology has changed the face of HRM in the Sri Lanka and abroad.  Perhaps the most central use of technology in HRM an organization is human resource information system (HRIS).

## Managing Change

Technology and globalization are only two of the forces driving change in organizations and HRM. As Jack Welch, CEO of General Electric put it, 'you' have got to be on the cutting edge of change. You cannot simply maintain the status quo, because somebody is always coming from another country with another product, or consumer tastes change, or the cost structure does, or there is technology break through. If you are not fast and adaptable, you are vulnerable. This is true for every segment of every business in every country in the world.

## Developing Human Capital

The idea that organization "compete through people" highlights the fact that success increasingly depends on an organization's ability to manage human capital. Human capital is an overall term used to describe the value of knowledge, skills, and capabilities that may not show up on a company's balance sheet but nevertheless have tremendous impact on an organization's performance.

Human Capital is intangible and elusive and cannot be managed the way organizations manage jobs, products, and technologies. One of the reasons for that employees are not own by the organization but their own human capital. If valued employees leave a company, they take their human capital with them, and any investment the company has made in training and developing those people is lost. To build human capital in organizations, managers must being to develop strategies for ensuring superior knowledge, skills, and experience within their workforce.

## Responding to the Market

Meeting customer expectations is essential for any organizations. Managers must have to meet customer requirements of quality, innovation, variety and responsiveness. These standards often separate the winners from the losers in today's competitive world. How well does company understand its customer's need? How fast can it develop and get a new product to market? How effectively has it responded to special concerns? "Better, faster, cheaper..." These standards require organizations to constantly align their processes with customer needs. Management innovations such as total quality management (TQM) and process reengineering are two of the comprehensive approaches to responding to customer. Each has direct implications for HR..

## 1.4.    Implementation of SHRM

The emergence of HRM has also highlighted the issue of the linkages between the employment relationship and wider organizational strategies and corporate policies the role of HRM has been reactive and supportive to other managerial functions.  HRM has come a long way to claim a rightful place alongside other core management roles.   The HRM perspective has claims that a range of organizational objectives have been arranged in a strategic way to enhance the performance of employees in achieving these goals.

Three approaches have been identified for implementing SHRM. They vary in the extent of involvement in the overall strategic management of the firm.

- At the lowest travel of involvement; to and accommodates the organization's strategic goals.
- At a higher level of involvement – there is a more interactive role in that HRM has input in the formulation of strategies, particularly with respect to implementation issues.
- At the highest level of involvement – there is full integration, in that HRM is linked to the strategic planning group and the various HR activities are linked as well

Dyer (1986) identifies specific contributions that HRM can make in strategy formulation.  There can be involvement in the assessment of various strategic alternatives in terms of feasibility and desirability.  The HRM function can provide input concern the availability of the required human resources (quantity, quality and skill mix) and the costs of acquiring, retaining, developing and motivating such resources.

### 1.4.1.    Global Human Resource Management

The growing competitiveness in the global arena has forced companies to seek to gain competitive advantage in any possible way. Moreover, according to Porter (1980) the more difficult it is for competitors to imitate quickly such sources of competitive advantage, the higher the value of that source is. For this reason, it is argued that the management of human resources constitutes one of the more innovative sources compared to the traditional and less significant ones such as capital, technology and location (Bartlett and Ghoshal, 1991).

Many years there has been increasing international competition, and today most large organizations in the US, Europe and Japan function in a global economy.  A revolution in management practices, and increased emphasis on quality of work life (QW) has occurred over the same years In order to compete internationally, many overseas facilities must be established, with the effect that two general concerns are being addressed by many American and European companies, firstly, how does one manage a company's citizens working overseas?  Secondly, how the organizational management policies and practices in other cultures differ from those in the respective home countries?

The foremost challenges for firms going overseas is the need to select and train individuals who are able to work in a foreign culture.  Therefore programmes featuring international management and cross-culture training have increased in value.

More and more business executives recognise the importance of an effective people management for both the short and the long-term competitiveness and survival of the firm. The ability to attract, develop and motivate people is even more crucial when companies globalise and set up overseas subsidiaries, international HRM consists of the same main dimensions as domestic HRM, but there is more complexity in strategically coordinating the different organizational units across national barriers. While there has to be some degree of strategic integration among the HRM practices of the parent company and the subsidiary, there is also the need for MNCs to be aware of the different national contexts and be flexible and responsive to the local needs and conditions (Bartlett and Ghoshal 1991).

Also related to the issue of managing one's citizens in a foreign setting is the problem of adequate compensation for them.  This arises out of the volatility of major foreign currencies, particularly the US dollar. Corporations are meeting this challenge, therefore, by paying allowances for housing, payment of tax if required, education of the managers children, cost of living adjustments etc.,

For a firm to be competitive these days its HRM function must be characterized by:

1.   Transnational scope – going beyond a simple national or regional perspective and making human resources decisions with a global perspective.
2.   Transnational representation – globally competitive organizations must have multinational representation among their managerial employees.
3.   Transnational process – a decision making process that involves representative and ideas from a variety of cultures.

## 1.4.2.   Change Management

Every manager needs a clear understanding of how to manage change effectively.  Think of yourself in a managerial role, either present or past. You would have had the challenge of managing change some time or the other in your work life. According to Bateman and Snell (1999) organizational change is managed effectively when:

1. The organization is moved from its current state to some planned future state that will exist after the change.
2. The functioning of the organization in the future state meets expectations: that is, the change works as planned.
3. The transition is accomplished without excessive cost to the organization.
4. The transition is accomplished without excessive cost to individual organizational members.

People are the key to successful change. It is the people that will finally determine the fate of the organization. Whether an organization is poised to be great or just to survive, people have to care about its fate, and perceive how they can contribute. The entire organization should involve in a change.

### 1.4.3. Motivating People to Change

You have probably observed that people usually resist change and must be motivated to embrace it. As a manager, your efforts at such motivation will only succeed if you understand why people often resist change.

Energy theories refer to Newton's second law of thermodynamics. It states that in any random transaction, the entropy will increase. Entropy is a measure of how random things are – in other words, how chaotic. This implies that throughout the universe, any random change will be in the direction of increasing variety and complexity. It should be clear to you that if a manager doesn't do anything, the organization will change anyway. Therefore, managers need to be vigilant to intervene when the effect of the random change is detrimental.

Some reasons are general and arise in most change efforts while others relate to the specific nature of a particular change. Let us first see what the general reasons are. These arise regardless of the actual content of the change (Bateman and Snell 1999): such as Inertia, Timing, Surprise and Peer pressures.

According to Bateman and Snell (1999), other causes of resistance arise from the specific nature of a proposed change. Change-specific reasons for resistance stem from what people perceive to be the personal consequences of the change. Some of these reasons are:

Self-interest Most people care less about the organization's best interest than they do about their own best interests. They will resist a change if they think it will cause them to lose something of value.

Misunderstanding Even when the management proposes a change that will benefit everyone, people may resist because they don't fully understand its purpose. Different Assessments Employees receive different and usually less information than management receives. Such discrepancies cause people to develop different assessments of proposed changes.

*****

# 2  EMPLOYEE RESOURCING

## 2.1.  Employee resourcing strategy

Every firm would like to achieves competitive advantage by attracting and retaining more capable people than its rivals and employing them more effectively. Strategic HRM emphasizes the importance of human resources in achieving organizational capability and therefore the need to find people whose attitudes and behaviour are likely to be congruent with what management believes to be appropriate and conducive to success.

Employee resourcing is concerned with any means available to meet the needs of the firm for certain skills and behaviours. A strategy to enlarge the skill base may start with recruitment and selection but would extend into learning and development to enhance skills and modify behaviours, and methods of rewarding people for the acquisition of extra skills. Performance management processes can be used to identify development needs and motivate people to make the most effective use of their skills.

The HRM approach to resourcing therefore emphasizes that matching resources to organizational requirements does not simply mean maintaining the status quo and perpetuating a moribund culture. It can and often does mean radical changes in thinking about the skills and behaviours required in the future to achieve sustainable growth and cultural change. It also means using a systematic approach, starting with job analysis, job design, human resource planning and proceeding through recruitment, selection and induction, followed by performance management, learning and development, recognition and reward.

## 2.1.1. Job and Job analysis

A job consists of a group of related activities and duties. Ideally, the duties of a job should consist of natural units of work that are similar and related. They should be clear and distinct from those of other jobs to minimize misunderstanding and conflict among employees and to enable employees to recognize what is expected of **them.**

Process of Job analysis

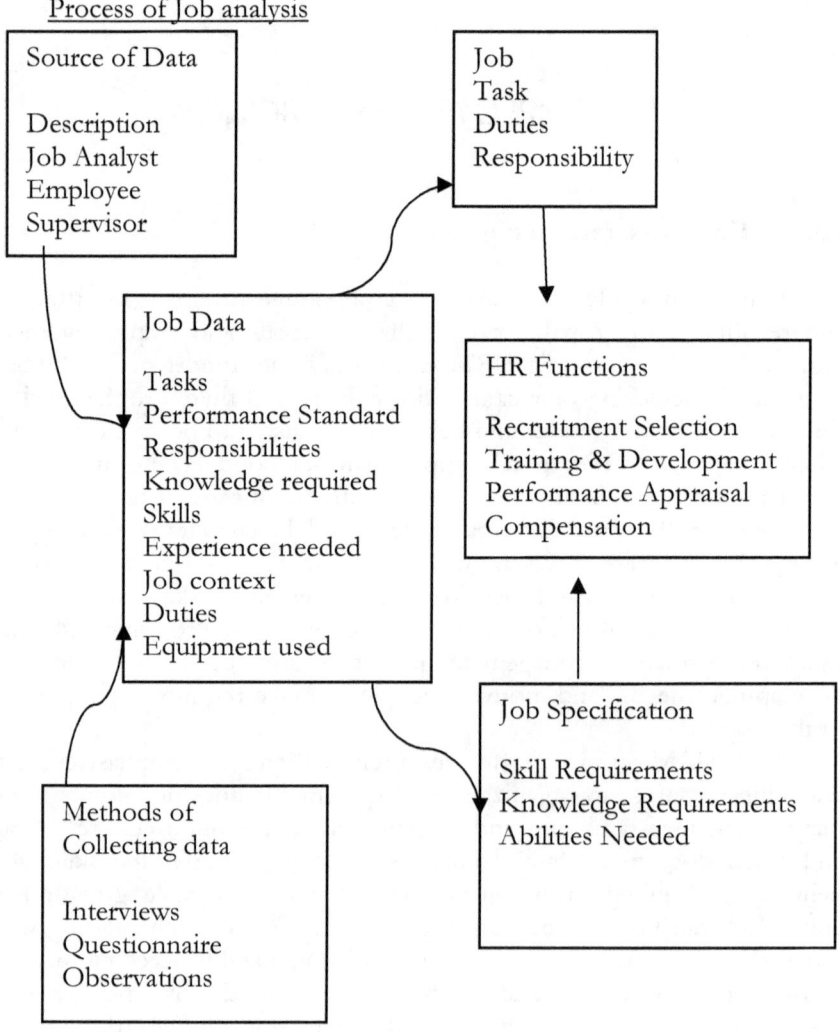

Figure 3.1 Job Analysis process

Process of Job analysis is obtaining information about jobs by determining what duties, tasks, or activities of jobs. HR managers will use these data to develop job descriptions and job specifications. Job analysis documents will be used to perform and enhance the different HR functions. The ultimate purpose of job analysis is performed, including the functions for which it is used.

"Job analysis is the process of collecting, analyzing and setting out information about the content of jobs in order to provide the basis for a job descriptions and data for recruitment, training, job evaluation and performance management. Job analysis concentrates on what job holders are expected to do" (Armstrong, 1999)

## Steps in Job Analysis

Step -1: Identify the use to which the information will be put, since this will determine the types of data you collect and how you collect them.

Step – 2: Review relevant background information such as organization charts, process charts, and job descriptions.

Step – 3: Select representative positions to be analyzed.

Step – 4: Actually analyze the job by collecting data on job activities, required employee behaviours, working conditions, and human traits and.abilities needed to perform the job.

Step – 5: Review the information with job incumbents. The job analysis information should be verified with the worker performing the job and with his or her immediate supervisor.

Step – 6: Develop a job description and job specification

Conducting job analysis is usually the primary responsibility of the HR department. Staff members of the HR division who specialize in job analysis have the title of job analyst or personnel analyst. Since the job carrying this title requires a high degree of analytical ability and writing skills.

## Gathering job information

Interviews - Job analyst may question individual employees & managers about job.

Questionnaire – The job analyst may circulate carefully prepared questionnaires to be filled out individually by jobholders & managers.

Observation – The analyst may learn about the jobs by observing and recording on a standardized form the activities of job holders.

Diaries - Job holders themselves may be asked to keep a diary of them work activities during an entire work cycle.

## 2.2.    Job Description and Job Specification

Job description is a Statement of the tasks, duties, and responsibilities of a job are to be performed.   There is no standard format for job descriptions; they tend to vary in appearance and content from one organization to another.   However most of job descriptions will contain at least three parts. Such as the job title, Job identification section and Job duties section.

This description helpful managers recruitment, interview and orient a new employee. Job descriptions are of value to both the employees and the employer.

From the employee' stand point, job descriptions can be used to help them learn their job duties and to remind them of the results are expected to achieve.

From the employers stand point, written job descriptions can serve as a basis for minimizing the misunderstanding that occur between managers and their subordinates concerning job requirements.   They also establish management's right to take corrective action when the duties covered by the job description are not performed as required.

## Job Title

Selection of a job title is important for several reasons. The job title is of psychological importance, providing status to the employee. E.g. Sanitation engineer is a more appealing title than garbage collector.

If possible, the title should provide some indication of what the duties of the job entail. E.g.  Meat inspector, Electronic assembler, Sales person & Engineer.

The job title also should indicate the relative level occupied by its holder in the organizational hierarchy.   E.g. Junior Engineer, Welder's helper & Laboratory assistant.

### Job Identification

Usually follows the job title. It includes such items as the departmental location of the job, the person to whom the jobholders reports, and the date the job description was last revised.

Sometimes it also contains a payroll or code number, the number of employees performing the job, the number of employees in the department where the job is located. Statement of the job usually appears at the bottom of this section and serves to distinguish the job from others jobs.

### Job duties or essential functions

Statements covering job duties are typically arranged in order of importance. These statements should indicate the weight or value f each duty. Usually, but not always the weight of a duty can be limited by the percentage of time devoted to it. The statements should stress the responsibilities all the duties entail and the results they are to accomplish. It is also general practice to indicate the tools and equipment used by the employee in performing the job.

### Problems with job descriptions

Job description is a valuable tool for performing HRM functions. If they are poorly written, using vague rather than specific terms, they provide little guidance to the jobholders. They are sometimes not updated as job duties or specifications change. They may violate the law by containing specifications not related to job success. They can limit the scope of activities of the jobholder.

### Job Specifications

Establish the qualifications required of applicants for the job openings. Job specification provides a basis for attracting qualified applicants & discouraging unqualified ones. Skills relevant to a job include education or experience, specialized training, personal traits or abilities. The physical demands of a job refer to how much walking, standing, reaching lifting or talking must be done on the job.

The physical demands (Health, strength, age-range, body size, height, weight, voice).

Psychological features or special aptitudes including mental concentration, alertness, judgment and analytical ability.

Personal characteristics like appearance, leadership, initiative, emotional stability, drive, skill and dealing with others.

## *Job description of HR Manager*

| Job Title | : | HR Manager |
| Division | : | Site A |
| Dept | : | HR Director |
| Job Analyst | : | HR officer, Safety officer |

*Overall purpose of Jobs:*
*Within the limit of company HR policies, to provide a full HR services to line Management and to provide a frame work for maintaining good relationship between management and staff.*
*Principal responsibilities:*
  a)  *Ensure the efficient recruitment of suitable and sufficient staff to meet vacancies identified by departmental management.*
  b)  *Implement the company's payment policy in accordance with laid down procedures.*
  c)  *Advise line managers on employee relations and legal matters during negotiations with trade union representatives.*
  d)  *Establish and maintain a regular programme of joint consultation with employee representatives.*
  e)  *Ensure regular safety inspections.*
  f)  *Provide adequate training programmes for the induction of new staff, for job training and for supervisor training.*
  g)  *Advise departmental managers on management development matters.*
  h)  *Maintain adequate records for all staff.*
  i)  *Provide a routine health service for all employees.*
*Limits of Authority:*
*May commit company's financial resources for recruitment within agreed budgets.*
*May recruit own staff within budget limits.*
*May decide individual salary/wage levels in accordance with agree scales.*
*May suspend staff without pay increase of alleged serious misconduct.*
*Resources available:*
*Factory health centre*
*Security vehicles*
*Company car*

## Approaches to Job Analysis

*Functional Job Analysis (FJA)*

Quantitative approach to job analysis that utilizes a compiled inventory of the various functions or work activities that can make up and job and that assumes that each job involves three broad worker functions.

1) Data    2) People    3) Things

E.g. Receptionist-copy the data, speak with people and handle things. FJA can easily be used to describe the content of jobs and assist in writing job description and specifications. It was developed by the U.S Training and Employment service.

*Position Analysis Questionnaire (PAQ)*

It is a quantifiable data collection method covering 194 different work oriented tasks which, by means of a five – point scale seeks to determine the degree to which different tasks are involved in performing particular job.

*The Critical Incident Method*

Job analysis methods are identified by which important job tasks for job success.

## 2.2.1.   Job Design

Job design is a deliberate attempt to structure the technical and social aspects of work. It includes organizing the components of the tasks to be performed, and the interaction patterns among group members to get the job done. Job design includes specialization, job enlargement, work simplification, operation analysis and behavioral sciences. Employee satisfaction, motivation, maximum operational efficiency is the basic objectives of the process of job design.

An outgrowth of job analysis is that improves jobs through technological and human considerations in order to enhance organization efficiency and employee job satisfaction. Job design should facilitate the achievement of organizational objectives and, at the same time, the design should recognize the capabilities and needs of those who are to perform to it.

"the specification of the contents, methods, and relationships of jobs in order to satisfy technological and organizational requirements as well as the social and personal requirements of the jobholder" (Davis, 1966)

## Job Design Process

*Industrial Engineering*

A field of study concerned with analyzing work methods and establishing time standards.

*Ergonomics*

An interdisciplinary approach to designing equipment and systems that can be easily and efficiently used by human beings.

The aims of job design are to satisfy the needs of the organization for productivity, operational efficiency and quality of the product or service. To satisfy the needs of the individual for interest, challenge and achievement.

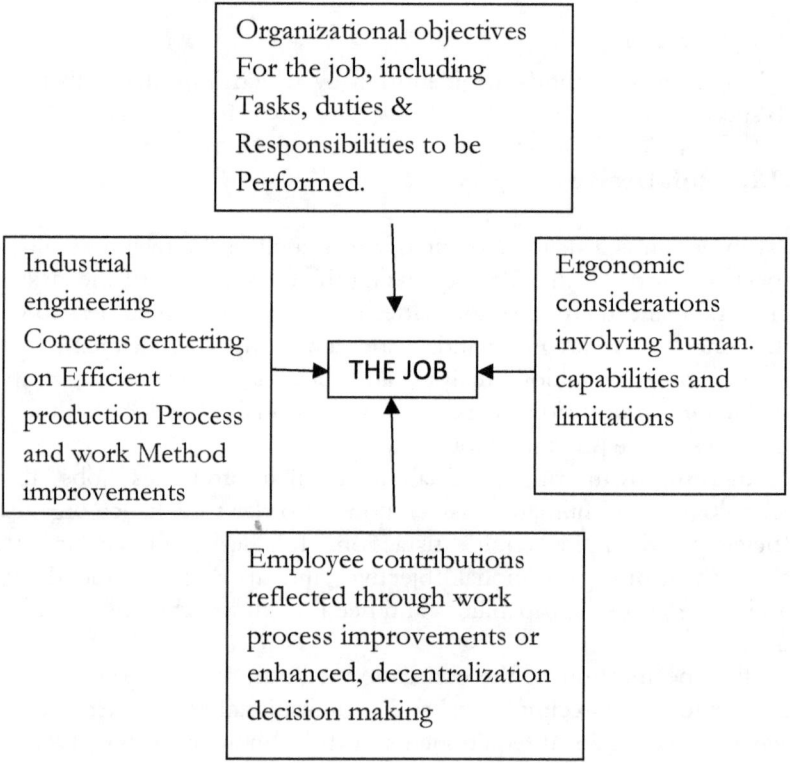

Figure 3.2 Process of Job Design

## Job Design involves the following decisions:

Designing a job involves making decisions as to who, what, where, when, why and how the job will be performed:

- Determining what tasks will be performed by the workforce.
- Determining the tasks to be grouped together and assigned to individuals.
- Determining how individuals will relate to one another so that work can be coordinated.
- Determining how they will be rewarded for their performance as members of the organization.

## Factors affecting Job Design:

- Changing technology
- Ability of present personnel
- Available supply of potential employees
- Psychological and social needs of human beings that can be met by the job.

**Job design Techniques** - There are five job design techniques:

- Job rotation: refers to the movement of employees from one task to another to reduce monotony and increasing variety.
- Job enlargement: refers to the combining of previously fragmented tasks into one job again, to increase variety in work.
- Job enrichment: refers to adding greater autonomy and responsibility to a job on the basis of its characteristics.
- Self-managing teams: these are groups that work together largely without direct supervision. They are given discretion over how work is done.
- High-performance work design: refers to the context where organizations require environments with high levels of performance.

## 2.3.    Human Resource Planning (HRP)

Human resource can contribute to an organization's competitive advantage more than any other resource. Look at the leading organizations in the world, why are they competitive? They have competent, well trained and motivated human resources. They need to be planned for their effective contribution.

HRP determines the human resource required by the organization to achieve its goals. As defined by Bulla and Scott (1994), it is a process for

27

ensuring that the human resource requirements of an organization are identified and plans are made for satisfying those requirements. Human Resource planning is based on the belief that people are an organization's most important strategic resource. It is generally concerned with matching resources to business needs in the long term, although it will sometimes address shorter term requirements. It addresses human resource needs in both quantitative and qualitative terms, which means answering two basic questions: 1) How many people? And 2) what sort of people?

HRP is indeed concerned with broader issues about the employment of people than the traditional quantitative model approach of "Manpower Planning". But it specifically addresses those aspects of human resource management that are primarily about the organization's requirements for people from the viewpoint of numbers, skills and how they are deployed. "Employment planning is the process of formulating plans to fill future openings based on an analysis of the positions that are expected to be open and whether these will be filled by inside or outside candidates" (Dessler, 1997).

The systematic and continuing process of analyzing an organization's human resource needs under changing conditions and developing personnel policies appropriate to the longer-term effectiveness of the organization. It is an integral part of corporate planning and budgeting procedures since human resource costs and forecasts both affect and are affected by longer-term corporate plans" (CIPD, UK)

**Purpose of HRP**
- Its purpose is to deploy these resources as effectively as possible, where and when they are needed, in order to accomplish the organization's goals;
- Obtains and retains the number of people it needs with the skills, expertise and competences required.
- Anticipating labour shortages and surpluses.
- Make the best use of its resources
- Recruit sufficient and suitable staff, optimum utilization of staff, and improvement of staff performance.
- To identify trouble areas.
- To assist productivity bargaining

**Consequences of Inadequate HRP or Lack of HRP**
An organization may incur several intangible costs as a result of inadequate HRP. It is difficult for employees to make effective plans for career or personal development. As a result, some of them may seek other employment where they feel they will have better career opportunities.

### 2.3.1.   HRP and Strategic Planning

HRP integrate with Strategic planning. As organizations plan for their future, HR managers must be concerned with meshing HRP with strategic business planning. Successful HRP helps to increase the capacity of the organization to act and change in pursuit of sustainable competitive advantage.

HRP and Strategic Planning become effective when there is a reciprocal and interdependent relationship between them. In this relationship, the top management team recognizes the strategic planning decision affect and is affected by HR concerns.

As James Walker, noted HRP expert, put it, "Today, virtually all business issues have people implications; all human resource issues have business implications". In the best of companies such as Merck, Intel, and Xerox there is no distinction between strategic planning and HRP.

HR Managers are important facilitators of the planning process and are viewed as credible and important contributions to creating the organization's future. HR Manager becomes a member of the organization's management steering committee or strategic planning group.

Table 4.1 Illustrates basic outline of how companies begun aligning HRP and Strategic Planning.

| Strategic Analysis | Strategy Formulation | Strategy Implementation |
|---|---|---|
| Establish the context: | Clarify performance expectations future management methods. | Implement process to achieve desired results: |
| Business goals company strengths External opportunities and threats source of competitive advantage | Values, guiding principles Business mission Objectives and priorities Actions Plans Resource allocations | Organizational change Strategic staffing Learning and develop Employee relations Implement HR Processes |
| Identify people-related business issues | Define HR strategies, objectives and action plans | |

Source : James W. Walker, "Integrating the HR Function with the Business, 1996

29

## 2.3.2 Elements of Effective HRP

Key elements

- Forecasting the Daman for labour
- Performing supply analysis
- Balancing supply and demand considerations

### Human Resource Planning Model/Process

| Forecast Demand | Forecast Supply |
|---|---|
| Considerations | Internal |
| Product/service demand | Staffing |
| Economics | Markov analysis |
| Technology | Skill inventories |
| Financial Resources | Management inventories |
| Absenteeism/turnover | Replacement charts |
| Organizational growth | Succession Planning |
| Management philosophy | External |
| | Demographic changes |
| Techniques | Education of work force |
| Trend analysis | Labour mobility |
| Managerial estimate | Governmental policies |

Balance Supply and Demand

Recruitment (Shortages)

Full time

Part time

Recalls

Reduction (Surpluses)

Terminations

Layoffs

Demotions

Retirement

Careful attention to each factor will help top managers and super visors to meet their staffing requirements. A key component of HRP is forecasting the number and type of people needed to meet organizational objectives. A variety of organizational factors including competitive strategy, technology, structure and productivity, can influence the demand for labour, such as utilization of advanced technology is generally accompanied by less demand for low skilled workers and more demand for knowledge workers.

External factors: such as business cycle, economic and seasonal trends can also play a role. Forecasting is frequently more an art than a science, providing inexact approximations rather than absolute results.

The ever changing environment in which an organization operates contributes to this problem.

## 2.4. Approaches to HR Forecasting

### Quantitative Approaches

Quantitative approaches to forecasting involve the use of statistical or mathematical techniques.

I.       Trend Analysis

A quantitative approach to forecasting labour demand based on an organizational index such as sales. Trend analysis is a study of a firm's past employment needs over a period of years to predict future needs.

Steps
a)   Select an appropriate business factor Example: Sales, No. of Beds etc.,
b)   Plot a historical trend of the business factor in relation to No. of employees.
c)   Compute the productivity ratio for at least the past five years.

$$\text{Productivity} = \frac{\text{Business Factor}}{\text{Number of employees}}$$

d)   Calculate human resource demand by determining the business factor by the productivity ratio.

$$\text{HR demand} = \frac{\text{Business Factor}}{\text{Productivity Ratio}}$$

e)   Project HR demand out to the target year

II. Modeling/Multiple Predictive Techniques

Whereas trend analysis relies on a single factor to predict employee needs, the more advanced methods combine several factors such as Int. rate, sales, GNP and disposable income leads predict employee.

While the cost of developing these forecasting methods used to be quite high advances in technology and computer software are have made rather sophisticated forecasting tools affordable to even small businesses.

## *Qualitative Approaches*

In contrast to quantitative approaches, qualitative approaches to forecasting are less statistical, attempting to reconcile the interests, abilities, an aspiration of individual employees with the current and future staffing needs of an organization. In both large and small organizations, HR planners may rely on experts who assist in preparing forecasts to anticipate staffing requirements.

I. Management Forecasts/Managerial Estimates

The most typical method of forecasting used is managerial judgment. This simply requires managers to sit down, think about their future workloads, and decide how many people they need. The opinions of supervisors, department managers, other knowledgeable about the organizations future employment needs.

II. Delphi Techniques

Attempt to decrease the subjectivity of forecasts by soliciting and summarizing the judgments of a pre-selected group of individuals. The final forecast thus represents a composite group judgment. The Delphi technique requires a great deal of coordination and cooperation in order to ensure satisfactory forecasts. This method works best in organizations where dynamic technological changes affect staffing levels.

- Select group of experts
- Provide questionnaire
- Deal of coordination and cooperation

Ideally, HRP should include the use of both quantitative and qualitative approaches. In combination, the two approaches serve to complement each other, providing a more complete forecasts by bringing together the contributions of both theoretical and practitioners.

## 2.4.1. Forecasting Supply of Employees

Once an organization has forecasting its future requirements for employees, it must then determine if there are sufficient numbers and types of employees available to staff anticipated openings. Supply analysis can be applied to two requirement sources-internal and external.

## 1. Internal Labour Supply

a. Staffing tables:

This is pictorial representation of all organizational jobs, along with the number of employees currently occupying the jobs and future (Monthly or yearly) employment requirement.

b. Markov Analysis:

It is a method for tracking the pattern of employee movements through various jobs. Shows the percentage and actual No. of employees who remain in each job from one year to the next, as well as the proportions of those who are promoted, demoted, transferred, or exit the organization (terminated or retired).

c. Skill Inventories:

Can also be prepared that lists of each employee's personnel education, past work experience, vocational interests, specific abilities and skills, compensation history, and job tenure. Of course, confidentiality is vital concern in setting up any such inventory. Nevertheless, well-prepared and up to-date skill inventories allow an organization to quickly match forthcoming job openings with employees backgrounds.

d. Replacement Charts:

It is listing of current jobholders and persons who are potential replacements, if an opening occurs. This chart shows that how an organization might replacement for the managers in one of its divisions. And it will provide information on the current job performance and promo ability of possible replacements.

e. Succession Planning

This is a process of identifying, developing and tracking key individuals for executive positions.

The supply of HR is also dependent on the turnover and absenteeism of employees. The formulas for computing turnover and absenteeism rates are below.

## Employees Turnover Rates

Employee turnover refers to the movement of employees out of an organization. It is also one of the chief determinants of labour supply.

Even if everything else about an organization stays the same, as employees turn over, the supply of labour goes down. This involves both direct and indirect costs to the organization.

$$\text{Turnover Rate} = \frac{\text{Number of separations during the month}}{\text{Total number of employees at midmonth}} \times 100$$

Cost of turnover: Cost generally be broken down into three categories: separation costs for the departing employees, replacement costs, and training costs for the new employees.

### Employee Absenteeism Rates

How frequently employee are absent from their work – the absenteeism rate is also directly related to HR planning and recruitment. When employees miss work, the organization incurs direct costs of lost wages and decreased productivity. A certain amount of absenteeism is, of course, unavoidable. There will always be some who must be absent from work because of sickness, accidents, serious family problems or other legitimate reasons.

$$\text{Turnover rate} = \frac{\text{Number of worker-days lost through job absence during period}}{\text{(Average number of employees)* (Number of workdays)}} \times 100$$

## 2. External Labour Supply

When an organization lacks an internal supply of employees for promotions or when it is staffing entry-level positions, managers must consider the external supply of labour. Many factors influence labour supply, including demographic changes in the population, national and regional economics, and education level of the workforce, demand for specific employee skills, population mobility and government policies.

### Balancing Supply and Demand Consideration

HRP should strive for a proper balance not only between forecasting techniques and their application but also between the emphasis placed on demand considerations and that placed on supply consideration. Demand considerations are based on forecast trends in business activity. Supply considerations involve the determination of where and how candidates with the required qualifications are to be found to fill vacancies. Because of the difficulty in locating applicants for the increasing number of jobs that require advanced training, this aspect of planning is receiving more attention. Grater planning effort is also needed in recruiting members of protected classes for managerial jobs and technical jobs that required advanced levels of education.

### Downsizing

As a strategy is here to stay, it is part of larger goal of balancing staff to meet changing needs. When organizations become overstaffed, they will likely cut jobs. An activity in an organization aimed at creating greater efficiency by eliminating certain jobs.

### Rightsizing

Linking employee needs to organizational strategy. Organization likely to increase staff when doing so adds value to the organization.

### Outsourcing

Sending work outside the organization to be done by individuals not employed full time with the organization.

*****

# 3   RECRUITMENT AND SELECTION

## 3.1. Recruitment

Recruitment is the process of locating and encouraging potential applicants to apply for existing or anticipated job openings. During this process, efforts are made to inform the applicants fully about the qualifications required to perform the job and the career opportunities the organization can offer its employees. Employee recruiting means finding or attracting applicants for the employer's open positions (Dessler,2008).

Process of seeking and attracting a pool of people from qualified candidate for job vacancies can be chosen. In an era when the focus of most organizations has been on efficiently and effectively running the organizations, recruiting the right person for the job is a top priority.

Recruitment is "searching for and obtaining potential job candidates in sufficient numbers and quality so that the organization can select the most appropriate people to fill its job needs". (Dowling and Schuler 1990)

"Recruitment is the process of finding and employing individuals to carry out the tasks that need to be done within an organization" (Maund 2001)

### Why Recruiting is Important

Effective recruiting is increasingly important. barring some dramatic change, there will soon be an undersupply of workers. The bureau of labour statistics estimates the United States will have created 22 million new jobs between 2003 and 2010, but only about 17 million new entrants will join the workforce; several things could change this scenario.

Even high unemployment, as 2003 and 2009, doesn't necessarily mean that t is easy to find good candidates. A survey during that period y department of labour found that about half of respondents said they had difficulty to finding qualified candidates, about 40% aid it was hard to find good candidates. Effective recruiting is thus not just important when the unemployment rate is low.

Recruiting does not just involve placing ads and calling employment agencies. There are several things that make it more complex. First, recruitment efforts should make sense in terms of the company's strategic plans. Second we will see that some recruiting methods are superior to others, depending on the type of job you are recruiting for. Third, the success you have recruiting depends greatly on non-recruitment issues and policies. Fourth good recruiting preferably always requires simultaneously pre-screening employees. And last the firm's image affects its recruiting results and employment law prescribes what recruiter managers can and can't do.

### 3.1.1. Recruitment Process

A particular job vacancy will be filled by someone from within the organization or from outside will, of course, depend upon the availability of personnel, the organization's HR policies and the requirements of the job to be staffed.

Lager organization must decide that they will conduct all their recruiting from a central recruitment office, or decentralize recruiting to the company's various offices. There are advantages to centralizing recruitment, it makes easier to apply the company's strategic priorities and it reduces duplication, makes it easier to spread the cost of new technologies. On the other hand, if the company's divisions are autonomous, or their recruitment needs are varied, it may be more sensible to decentralize the recruitment process.

### Defining requirements

This is the first step in the recruitment process. At this initial stage, the organization is required to lay down the requirements for human resource, both quantitatively and qualitatively. The two main mechanisms for identifying and specifying requirements are the Job analysis and human resource planning. Therefore, the organization will now develop a recruitment plan that comes from the overall human resource plan. During the stage of defining requirements for human resources, managers have to be cautious not to overestimate the definition of recruitments.

In addition, there will be demands for replacements or for new jobs to be filled, and these demands should be checked to ensure that they are justified. Requirement for particular positions are set out in the form of role profiles and person specifications. These provide the basic information required to draft advertisements and assess candidates. A role profile listing competence, skill, educational and experience requirements produces.

## Attracting Candidates

Attracting candidates is primarily a matter of identifying, evaluating and using the most appropriate sources of applicants. In this stage , managers have to identify and evaluate the sources from which candidates can be attracted. However, in cases where difficulties in attracting or retaining candidates are being met or anticipated, it may be necessary to carry out a preliminary study of the factors that are likely to attract or repel candidates – the strengths and weaknesses of the organization as an employer.

## 3.2. Sources of Recruitment

### Internal Sources
If an organization has been effective in recruiting and selecting employees in the past, one of the best sources of talent is its own employees.

*Method of locating qualified candidates*
The effective use of internal sources requires a system for locating qualified job candidates and for enabling those who consider themselves qualified to apply for the opening.  Qualified job candidates within the organization can be located by computerized record systems, by job posting and bidding and Rehiring.
1.   Computerized Record System
Computers have made possible the creation of databanks that contain the complete records and qualifications of each employee within organizations.
2.   Job Position and bidding
Posting vacancy notices and maintaining lists of employees looking for upgraded positions. Job posting means publicizing the open job to employees, these list the jobs attributes, like qualifications, supervisor, work schedule and pay rate.
3.   Rehiring
Former employees are known quantities, and are already familiar with the company's culture, syle, way of doing things. On other hand, employees who were let go may return with less than positive attitudes.

Hiring former employees who resigned back into better positions may signal current employees that the best way to get ahead is to leave the firm.

*Advantages of Recruiting by Internal:*

Most organizations try to follow a policy of filling job vacancies above the entry-level position through promotions and transfers.

1. Organizations can capitalize on the investment it has made in recruiting, selecting, training, and developing its current employees. Full use of the abilities of the organization's employees improves the organization's return on its investment.
2. Promotions contribute to the companies' overall growth and success. Promotions serve to reward employees for past performance and are intended to encourage them to continue their efforts. It also gives other employees reason to anticipate that similar efforts by them will lead to promotions, thus improving morale within the organization.
3. Organizations have good idea of the strength and weakness of its employees.
4. More accurate data are available concerning current employees, thus reducing the chance of making a wrong decision.
5. Employee knows more about the organization and how it operates.
6. Employee motivation and morale.

*Disadvantages of recruiting by Internal:*

1. Negative effect on the morale and performance of people who are not promoted.
2. Inbreeding of ideas-New ideas innovations are not stifled by such attitudes as "We have never done it before" or "We do all right without it".

## External Sources

External recruiting is needed in organizations that are growing rapidly or have a large demand for technical, skilled, or managerial employees. The outside sources from which employers recruit will vary with the type of position to be filled.

Eg. A computer programmer is not likely to be recruited from the same source as machine operator. The condition of the labour market may also help to determine which recruiting sources an organization will use. During periods of high unemployment, organizations may be able to maintain an adequate supply of qualified applicants from unsolicited resume alone. A tight labour market, one with low unemployment, may force the employer to advertise heavily and or seek assistance from local employment agencies.

*Advantages of recruiting by external*
1. Pool of talent is much larger than that available from internal sources.
2. Can bring new insights and perspectives to the organization.
3. Cheaper and easier to hire technical, skilled, or managerial people from the outside rather than training and developing them internally.

*Disadvantages of external recruitment*
1. Attracting, contacting, evaluating potential employees is more difficult.
2. Need a longer adjustment or orientation period.
3. May cause morale problems among people within the organization who feel qualified.

### 3.2.1 Methods of Recruitment

#### Advertisement
One of the most common methods of attracting applicants is through advertisements. While newspapers and trade journals are the media used most often, radio, TV, billboards, posters and email are also utilized. Advertising has the advantage of reaching a large audience of possible applicants. While web-based recruiting is rapidly replacing help wanted ads, a glance at almost any paper or business or professional magazine will confirm that print ads are still popular. To success ads, employers have to address two issues: the advertising medium and the ads construction.

#### Employment Agencies
There are three main types of employment agencies: Public, nonprofit organization and private agencies, Charging a fee enables private employment agencies to tailor their services to the specific needs of their clients. It is common for agencies to specialize in serving a specific occupational area or professional field.

#### Executive search firms
In contrast to public and private employment agencies, which help job seekers find the right job, executive search firms (often called "headhunters") help employers find the right person for a job. They seek out candidates with qualifications that match the requirements of the positions their client firm is seeking to fill.

### Educational Institutions

Educational institutions typically are a source of young applicants with formal training but with relatively little full-timework experience. High schools and colleges in Sri Lanka are usually a source of employees for clerical. For technical and managerial positions, campuses and universities are generally the primary source. However, the suitability of university graduates for open positions often depends on their major field of study.

### Employee Referrals

The recruitment efforts of an organization can be aided by employee referrals, or recommendations made by current employees. Managers have found that the quality or employee-referred applicants is normally quite high, since employees are generally hesitant to recommend individuals who might not perform well.

### Unsolicited Applications and Resumes

Many employers receive unsolicited applications and resumes from individuals may or may not be good prospects for employment. Even through the percentage of acceptable applicants from this source may not be high, a source cannot be ignored.

### Professional Organizations

Many professional organizations and societies offer a placement service to members as one of their benefits. Listings of members seeking employment may be advertised in their journals or publicized at their national meetings.

### Labour Unions

Labour unions can be a principal source of applicants for blue collar and some professional jobs. Employees wishing to use this recruitment source should contact the local union under consideration for employer eligibility requirements and applicant availability.

### Temporary help agencies

People working for employment agencies, who are subcontracted out to businesses at an hourly rate for a period of time specified by the businesses.

## Effectiveness of Recruitment Methods

Organizational recruitment programs are designed to bring a pool of talent to the organizational. From this pool, the organization hopes to select the person or persons most qualified for the job. An obvious and very important question faced by HR department is which method or re recruitment supplies the best talent pool.

Many studies have explored this issue. One study concluded that employee referrals were private employment agencies, and walk-in applicants. This study found that turnover rates for employees hired from employee referrals were lower than for employees hired through the other methods.

Other study found that only about 44% of the 279 firms surveyed made formal attempts to evaluate the outcomes of their recruitment efforts. What to measure and how to measure of recruiting effectiveness is that how many applicants we generated through each of our recruitment sources. If more applicants are generated than there are positions to fill, the firm can be more selective. The problem is that more is not always better; the employer needs qualified, hireable applicants, not just applicants.

How to measure each recruiting source's effectiveness is to asses applicants from each source using simple pre-screening selection devices. Having assessed the quality of each recruitment source, the employer may then want to redirect recruiting from sources that produce more applicants but lower quality ones to sources that produce fewer but better candidate.

## 3.3. Selection

Selection is the process of choosing individuals who have relevant qualifications to fill existing or projected job openings. With increased emphasis on the human side of competitiveness, making correct hiring decisions is of crucial importance.

Job analysis, HRP, and recruitment are prerequisites to the selection process. A break down in any of the processes can make even the best selection system ineffective.

Selection is the last part of the recruitment process when the organization decides who to employ from the candidates available. ( Maund 2001).

According to Dessler (1997), selection is important for three reasons that performance, cost and legal implications.

The purpose of selection is to distinguish individuals who perform from those who don't. Hence, is vital for selectors and human resource managers to identify key elements in individuals that can predict the best behaviour and performance after they have been employed.

Although costs relating to selecting individuals may not appear to be exorbitant, there are several expenses that can make the selection unduly costly.

The selection process and its resultant decisions are often exposed to legal implications. Employing an individual with past criminal records can lead to serious financial and legal obligations.

### 3.3.1 Selection Process

Processing an applicant for a job normally entails a series of steps. Figure 6.1 illustrates the steps in typical selection process.

*Steps in the selection process*
1. Completion of application form
2. Initial interview in HR department
3. Employment test/formal testing
4. Background investigation/Reference checking
5. Interview
6. Medical examination/physical examination
7. Hiring decision/selection decision

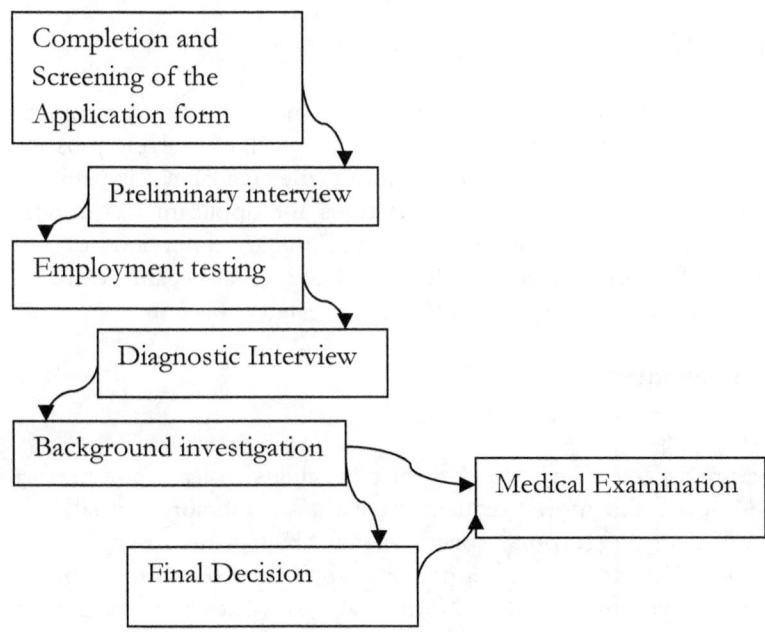

Figure 3.1 : Steps in the selection process

### Application Form

Completing an application form is normally the first steps in most selection procedures. The application provides basic employment information for in later steps of the selection process and can be used to screen out unqualified applicants. E.g. If the job openings requires the ability to sue a word processor and the applicant indicates and in ability to use a word processor, there is no need to process the application further.

Purpose of application form

1.      They provide information for deciding whether an applicant meets the minimum requirements for experience education, etc.
2.      They provide a basis for questions the interviewer will asks applicant's background.
3.      They also offers sources for reference check.

*Suggestions for putting together an application form*

1.      Application Date
2.      Educational background
3.      Experience
4.      Arrest and criminal convictions
5.      Country of citizenship
6.      References
7.      Disability

## Preliminary Interview

The preliminary interview is used to determine whether the applicant's skills, abilities, and job preference match any of the available jobs in the organization, to explain to the applicant the available jobs and then requirements, and to answer any questions the applicant has about the available jobs or the employer. A preliminary interview is usually conducted after the applicant has completed to applicant form. The interview screens out un qualified or un interested applicant.

## 3.3.2 Employment Tests

*1. Aptitude Tests*

Measure a person's capacity or potential ability to learn and perform a job. Some of the more frequently used tests measure verbal bailing, numerical ability, perceptual speed, spatial ability, and reasoning ability verbal aptitude tests measures a person's ability to use words in thinking, planning and communicating. Numerical assets measure ability to add, subtract, multiply and divide. Perception speed tests measure ability to recording similarities and references. Spatial tests measure ability to visualize objects in space determines their relationship.

Reasoning tests measure ability to analyse oral or written facts and make correct judgments concerning those facts on the basis of logical in implications.

*2. Psychomotor Tests*

Measure a person's strength, dexterity, and coordination. Finger dexterity, manual dexterity, wrist finger speed, and speed or movements are some of the psychomotor abilities that can be tested.

*3. Job Knowledge Test*

Measure the job related knowledge possessed by a job applicant. These tests can be either written or oral.

*4. Interest Tests*

Are designed to determine how a person's interests compare with the interest of successful people in a specific job. These tests indicate the occupations or areas of work in which the person is most interested.

*5. Personality Tests*

Attempt to measure personality characteristics these tests are generally characterized by questionable validity and low reliability and presently have limited use for selection purpose.

*6. Polygraph tests*

A device records physical changes in a person's body as he or she answers questions the polygraph records fluctuations in blood pressure & respiration on a moving roll of seraph paper.

*7. Graphology (handwriting analysis)*

To examine the times, loops, hooks, stores, curves, and flounces in a person's handwriting to assess the person's personality, performance, emotional problems, and honesty.

*8. Physical Ability Tests*

In addition to learning about a job candidate's mental capabilities, employer's frequently need to assess a person's physical abilities as well. Particular for demanding & optionally dangerous job we those hold by fire fighters and police hires, physical abilities such as strength & endurance that to be not only good predictors of performance.

*9. Job Sample Tests*

Job sample tests or work sample tests require the applicant to perform test that are actually a part of the work required on the job.

## 3.4. Methods of Selection

Traditionally the employment interview has had a very important role in the selection process – so much, so that it is rare to find an instance where an employee is hired without some sort of interview. Depending upon the type of job, applicants may be interviewed by one person, by members of a work team, or other individuals in the organization. While researches have raised some doubts about its validity, the interview remains a mainstay of selection because (1) it is especially practical when there are only a small number of applicants, (2) if serves other purpose, such as public relations, and (3) interviews maintain great faith and confidence in their judgments. Nevertheless, the interview can be plagued by problems of subjectively and personal bias.

## Guidelines for Employment Interview

Organization should exercise considerable caution in the selection of employment interviewers. Qualities that are desirable include humility; ability to think objectively; freedom from over talkativeness, extreme opinions, and biases; maturity; and poise. A training program should be provided on a continuing basis for employment interviewers and at least periodically for managers and supervisors in other departments.

## 3.4.1 Interviews Methods/Types of interviews

Employment or selection interviews differ according to the methods used to obtain information and to find out an applicant's attitudes and feelings. The most significant difference lies in the amount structure, or control, exercised by the interviewer.

**Methods**
Structured Interview
Unstructured Interview
Situational Interview
Behavioural Description Interview
Stress Interview
Board or Panel Interview
Computer Interview
Job Related Interview

### Structured Interview

An interview in which have been prepared a set of standardized questions having an established set of answers is used. This method is particularly useful when interviewers find limited time to spend on interviews. Structured interviews may not leave way for much flexibility.

### Unstructured Interview

An interview conducted without predetermined checklist of questions. They use open ended questions such as "Tell me about your previous job". The purpose of this type of interview is to build up areas of interest so that more specific questions can be drawn up.

### Situational Interview
An Interview in which has developed a hypothetical incident is given to an applicant and asked how he or she would respond to it. The applicant's response is then evaluated relative to pre established benchmark standards.

### Behavioural Description Interview (BDI)
Similar to situational interview focuses on real work incidents. An interview in which an applicant is asked questions about what he or she actually did in a given situation. However, while a situational interview addresses hypothetical situations, the BDI format asks the job applicant what he or she actually did in a given situation.

### Stress Interview
This an interview where the candidate is made to feel uncomfortable by questions that are tough or rude. The purpose of this interview is to identify the tolerance level of candidates.

### Panel Interview
Another type of interview involves a panel of interviewers who question and observe a single candidate. In a typical panel interview, the candidate meets with three to five interviewers who take turns asking questions. After the interview, the interviewers pool their observations to reach a consensus about the suitability of the candidates.

### Computer Interview
Recently, a growing number of organizations have begun using computers to help with the interviewing process. The system asks candidates 75 to 125 MCQ tailored to the job and then compares the applicant's responses either with an ideal profile or with profiles developed on the basis of the candidate's responses. The computer can generate a printed report that contains the applicant's responses summary.

### Job related interview
A series of job-related questions which focuses on relevant past job related behaviours.

Guide rules for employment interviews
Establish an interview panel
Establish and maintain rapport
Be an active listener
Pay attention to nonverbal cues
Provide information as freely and honestly as possible
Use questions effectively

Separate facts from inferences
Recognize biases and stereotypes
Control the course of the interview
Standardize the questions asked

## Background Investigations

When the interview is satisfied that the applicant is potentially qualified, information about previous employment as well as other information provided by the applicant is investigated. Former employers, school, and college official, campus, university, and individuals named as references may be contracted for verification of pertinent information such as length of time on job, type of job, performance evaluation, highest wages, academic degrees earned and possible criminal record. Most of this information is now readily available on existing computer database.

Medical Examinations

The medical examination is one of the later steps in the selection process because it can be costly. A medical examination is generally given to ensure that the health of an applicant is adequate to meet the job requirements. It also provides a baseline against which subsequent medical examinations can be compared and interpreted.

## 3.4.2 Selection Decision

While all of the steps in the selection process are important, the most critical step is the decision to accept or reject applicants. Fundamentally, an employer is interested in what an applicant can do and will do. An evaluation of candidates on the basis of assembled information should focus on these two factors. The "can-do" factors include knowledge and skills, as well as the aptitude (the potential) for acquiring new knowledge and skills. The "will do" factors include motivation, interests, and other personality characteristics. Both factors are essential to successful performance on the job. The employee who has the ability (can do) but is not motivated to use it (will not do) is little better than the employee who lacks the necessary ability.

It is much easier to measure what the individuals can do than what they will do. The can do factors are readily evident from test scores and verified information. What the individual will do can only be inferred. Responses to interview and application form questions may be used as a basis for obtaining information for making inferences about what an individual will do.

## Decision Strategy

The strategy used for making personnel decisions for one category of jobs may differ from that used for another category. The strategy for selecting managerial and executive personnel, for example, will differ from that used in selecting clerical and technical personnel. While many factors are to be considered in hiring decisions, the following are some of the questions that managers must consider.

- Should the individuals be hired according to their highest potential or according to the needs of the organization?
- At what grade or wage level should the individual be started?
- Should initial selection be concerned primarily with an ideal match of the employee to the job, or should potential for advancement in the organization be considered?
- To what extent should those who are not qualified but are qualifiedly be considered?

## Approaches to selection

In addition to these types of factors, managers must also consider which approach they will use in making hiring decisions. There are two basic approaches to selection: Clinical and Statistical.

### Clinical approach (Personal Judgment)

In the clinical approach to decision making, those making the selection decision review all the data on applicants. Then, based on their understanding of the job and the individuals who have been successful in that job, they make decision. Different individuals often arrive at different decision about an applicant when they use this approach because each evaluator assigns different weights to the applicant's strengths and weaknesses.

### Statistical Approach

In contrast to the clinical approach, the statistical approach to decision making is more objective. It involves identifying the most valid predictors and weighting them through statistical methods such as multiple regressions. Quantified data such as scores or ratings from interview, tests, and other procedures are then combined according to their weighted value. Individuals with highest combined scores are selected.

## 3.5. Induction/ Orientation

In many instances, when employees report for work on the first day, there is hardly any advice given to them regarding how to get about the job, what pitfalls should be avoided, and in general what the company expects him/her to do in the job. In short, has there been some kind of orientation? Let us look at a definition.

Orientation is the personnel activity which introduces new employees to the enterprise and to their tasks, superiors, and work groups.

Armstrong has referred to the process of introducing the new employee as induction. He has defined induction as "the process of receiving and welcoming employees when they first join a company and giving them the basic information they need to settle down quickly and happily start work".

Orientation has not been studied a great deal, and little scientific research has been done on whether the programmes are adequate. The nature of the employee and the nature of the task, the work group, and the leadership are all important features of an effective orientation programme. The nature of the employee and the task are critical factors. For example, managers are given more detailed orientation programme

than other employees. The orientation programme focuses on introducing the new employer to the task, the work group, and the supervisor-leader. During orientation, the work policies of the organisation, the job conditions, and the other employees the new employee has to work with to get the job done are discussed.

The style it uses to orient new employees varies from organisation to organisation. The style is generally affected by the organisation and its operating climate. What are called conservative organisations will orient employees quite differently than liberal organisations will.

Selecting employees doesn't guarantee they will perform effectively. Potential is one thing, performance is another. Even high potential employees can't do their jobs if they don't know what to do or how to do it. Therefore all managers have to ensure that your employees do know what to do and how to do it.

### 3.5.1 Purposes of Orientation

Employee orientation provides new employees with the basic background information they need to work in the company. Employers have to consider the Induction and Orientation of new employees for the following reasons:

a) The introduction stage of the new employee has to be smooth because everything is strange and unfamiliar to them.

b) The employer has to act quickly to instill a favorable image of the organization in the mind of the new employee not only enabling but also to motivate them to remain in the organization.

c) The employer recruits the new employee for performance. Effective introduction leads to effective performance.

d) Introduction of new employee gives the first impression of the organization. An effective and memorable programme can minimize the chances of them to leaving the organization.

Orientation programs are moving away from more discussions of rules, to explaining the company's mission and employee's role in accomplishing it. The assumption is that this will foster self directed behaviour that is more consistent with the company's needs. An effective orientation programme

serves a number of purposes. In general, the orientation process is similar to what sociologists call socialization. The principal purposes of orientation are as follows:

### Reduce the start-up costs for a new employee:

In most instances, the new employee does not know the job, how the organisation works, or whom to see to get the job done. In fact he/she is a sort of a stranger to the organisation. This means that for a while, the new employee is less efficient than the experienced employee, and additional costs are involved in getting the new employee started. These start-up costs vary depending on the level of the employee; in the case of top managers it will cost much more than for lower grades of staff. Effective orientation reduces these start-up costs and enables the new employee to reach standards sooner.

### Reduce the amount of anxiety and hazing a new employee experiences:

Anxiety in this case means fear of failure on the job. Hazing takes place when experienced employees 'kid' the new employee. For example, experienced employees may ask the new worker, 'How many toys are you producing/per hour?' When the employee answers, he/she is told, 'You'll never last. The last one who did that few lasted only two days

the military, the situation may be more devastating to a new recruit. Such hazing serves several purposes. It lets the recruit know he has a lot to learn and thus is dependent on the others for his job, and it is 'fun' for the old-timers. But it can cause great anxiety for the recruit. Effective orientation alerts the new person to hazing and reduces anxiety.

### Reduce employee turnover:

If employees perceive themselves to be ineffective, unwanted, or unneeded, they may seek to deal with these negative feelings by quitting. Turnover is high during the break-in period, and effective orientation can reduce this costly condition.

**Save time for supervisor and co-workers:**

Improperly oriented employees must still get the job done, and to do so they need help. The most likely people to provide this help are the co-workers and supervisors, who will have to spend time breaking in new employees. Good orientation programmes save everyone time.

**Develop realistic job expectations, positive attitudes toward the employer, and job satisfaction:**

In what sociologists call the older professions or total institutions the job expectations are clear because they have been developed over long years of training and education. Society has built up a set of attitudes and behaviours that are considered proper for these jobs. For most of the world of work, however, this does not hold true. New employees must learn realistically what the organisation expects of them, and their own expectations of the job must be neither too low nor too high. Each worker must incorporate the job and its work values into his or her self-image.

Don't underestimate orientation's importance. Without basic information on things like rule and policies, new employees may make time consuming or even dangerous errors. Furthermore, orientation is not just about rules. It is also about making the new employee feel welcome and at home and part of the team.

### 3.5.2 Who Orients Employees

In general, orientation is a joint effort between operating managers and representatives of the personnel department. The personnel department usually introduces new employees to the organisation, handles the paper work of getting them enrolled in the organisation, puts them on the pay rolls, explains personnel policies regarding pay, benefits, and work rules. It also may develop an orientation checklist and brief the employees on their supervisor's expectations.

The operating manager or supervisor explains the task to the new employees. He or she shows them around the workplace and introduces them to other employees. The supervisor also explains what is expected in the way of job performance and work rules. Better supervisors usually alert present employees about the hiring of new employees and encourage them to help the recruits and welcome them to the work group. In some unionised organisations, trade union officials also take part in orienting new employees.

### 3.5.3 How Orients Employees

Orientation programmes vary from quite informal, primarily verbal efforts to formal schedules that supplement verbal presentations with written handouts. Formal orientations often include a tour of the facilities, or slides, charts, and pictures of them. Usually, they are used when a large number of employees must be oriented.

During induction, the Human Resource Manager or HR Specialist handles the Introductory. it is sometimes followed by an introduction to the new employee's supervisor. Some of the other topics covered during a typical orientation session are a presentation of the exact nature of the job, new employee's introduction to their colleagues and familiarizing them to the new environment.

- The formal programme usually covers such items as:
- History and general policies of the organisation
- Descriptions of the organisation's services or products.
- The way the organisation is structured.
- Safety measures and regulations.
- Personnel policies and practices.
- Compensation, benefits, and employee services provided.
- Daily routine and regulations.

Glueck (1978) presents five guidelines for conducting an employee orientation:

a)  Orientation should begin with the most relevant and immediate kinds of information and then proceed to more general organisation policies.

b)  The most significant part of orientation is the human side giving new employees knowledge of what supervisors and co-workers are like, telling them how long it should take to reach standards of effective work, and encouraging them to seek help and advice when needed.

c)  New employees should be 'sponsored' or directed by an experienced worker or supervisor in the immediate environment who can respond to questions and keep in close touch during the early induction period.

d)  New employees should be gradually introduced to the people with whom they will work rather than given a superficial introduction to all of them on the first day. The object should be to help them get to know their co-workers and supervisors.

e)  New employees should be allowed sufficient times to get their feet on the ground before demands on them are increased.

You should keep in mind that orienting management trainees is a special activity. Most management trainees come direct from universities or colleges and have to adjust from that life to work life. There is little doubt that initial experiences with an organisation are important predictors of future managerial performance. Therefore, the first impressions received are important to career and employee development. It is crucial therefore that management trainee, as they are future leaders, are put under the supervision of a successful senior executive who can be a role model for the trainees, and who also wants to get the trainees off to a good start. It must be ensured that trainees would not have unpleasant experiences during the initial period because fast turnover may cause the organisation heavy losses.

As new employees do not know the organization and are wondering how an organization would treat them, managers have to take extra effort not only to conduct the orientation programme effectively but also to see that some of logistical arrangements work to perfection during the orientation.

**The front desk arrangements:**

Inform the new employees the reporting time and person to report. The tome must be arranged well in advance so that it does not clash with another event.

Inform the receptionist or other staff members of the arrival of new employee and make preparations for instructions and activities for the day. The organization should ensure that new employees should not be kept waiting.

**Documentation arrangements:**

While some documents may have to be collected from the employee, some other documents will have to be prepared and handed over to the new employee. The typical documents that the employee has to present are birth, educational and work experience certificates, etc. in addition to these, the employer may request the new employee take certain oaths as well as to owe allegiance. And also asked to signed contract, code of conduct, etc. the organization may have to prepare some other documents to be handed over to the new employee such as employee hand book, policy and procedure, etc.

**Face to face arrangements:**

A face to face oral presentation is necessary to give organization's message to new employees. An induction programme with briefing of key issues relating to the organization is strongly recommended. a forum for raising and answering questions and feedback makes the face to face session stronger helping the new employee being more confident about themselves.

### Introduction to work setting:

This is crucial, because new employees will always have apprehensions about where exactly they would work; the organization has to be straightforward in conveying this message clearly to the person concerned. The name of the immediate supervisor or team leader should be mentioned and introduced in person. The new employee's work schedule for the first day has to be clearly mentioned. The work location has to be shown to the new employee with specific information relating to entrance, exit, toilet, canteen and other areas. Ideally the new employee's immediate supervisor will introduce the workplace.

### Induction schedule:

The induction have to conduct every new employee before begins work not after. An organization can sometimes wait for sufficient number of new employees to join in order to conduct the programme. However, induction should take place as soon as possible after joining. Similarly, if there is a wide difference between the type of work and employees, the induction programme should address such difference sufficiently.

### Orientation Follow-up:

Having selected the new employees the next or the final phase of the orientation programme is the assignment of the new employee to the job. At this point, the supervisor is supposed to take over and continue the orientation. But as many instances have brought out, supervisors are busy people, and they can overlook some of the facts needed by the new employee to do a good job, however much the supervisor is well intentioned. One way to assure adequate orientation is to design a feedback system to control the programme.

### The Employee Handbook:

The employee handbook's contents represent legally binding employment commitments. These make it clear that statements of company policies, benefits, and regulations do not constitute the terms and conditions of an employment contract either expressed or implied.

*****

# 4 TRAINING AND DEVELOPMENT

## 4.1. Training

Training is a learning process that involves the acquisition of knowledge, skills and abilities are to be enhancing employee performance. Or the process of teaching new employees the basic skills they need to perform their jobs.

The term "Training is often using casually to describe most any effort initiated by an organization to foster learning among its members. However, many experts make distinct between training, which tends to be narrowly focused and oriented toward short-term performance concerns, and development, which tends to be, oriented more toward broadening an individual's skills for the future responsibilities. The two terms tend to be combined into single phrase – "training and development" to recognize the combination of activities used by organizations to increase the skill base of employees.

### Objectives of training

a) Develop the competencies of employees and improve their performance.
b) Help people to grow within the organization in order that, as far as possible, its future needs for human resources can e met from within;
c) Reduce the learning tie for employees starting in new jobs on appointment, transfer or promotion, and ensure that they become fully competent as quickly and economically as possible.

## Importance of training

Training has become increasingly vital to the success of modern organizations. Training plays central role in nurturing and strengthening these competencies and in this way has become part of the backbone of strategy implementation. In addition, rapidly changing technologies require that employees continuously hone their knowledge, skills, and abilities (KSAs) to cope with new processes and systems. Jobs that require little skill are rapidly being replaced by jobs that require technical, interpersonal, and problem solving skills. Training is important to:

a) New employees
b) Existing employees

New employees: is to bring their KSAs up to the level required for satisfactory performance.
Existing employees: additional training to acquire new knowledge and skills.

### 4.1.1 Training Process

The primary goal of training is to contribute to the organization's overall goals; training programs should be developed with an eye to organizational goals and strategies. Unfortunately, many organizations never make the connection between their strategic objectives and their training programs. As a result, much of an organization's investment can be wasted and these problems can directly affect organizational performance.

To make certain that investments in training and development have maximum impact on individual and organizational performance. A system approach involves four phases:

1. Need assessment
2. Program design
3. Implementation
4. Evaluation

### Conducting the needs assessment

Managers and HR staffs should say alert to the kinds of training that are needed, where they are needed, and which methods best will deliver needed KSAs to employees. If workers consistently fail to achieve productivity objectives, this might be a signal that training is needed. Likewise if organizations receive an excessive number of customer complaints, this too might suggest inadequate training. To make certain that training is timely and focused on priority issues, managers should approach need assessment systematically by utilizing the three different types of analysis organizational analysis, task analysis and person analysis.

Figure 4.1: The Process of Training and Development

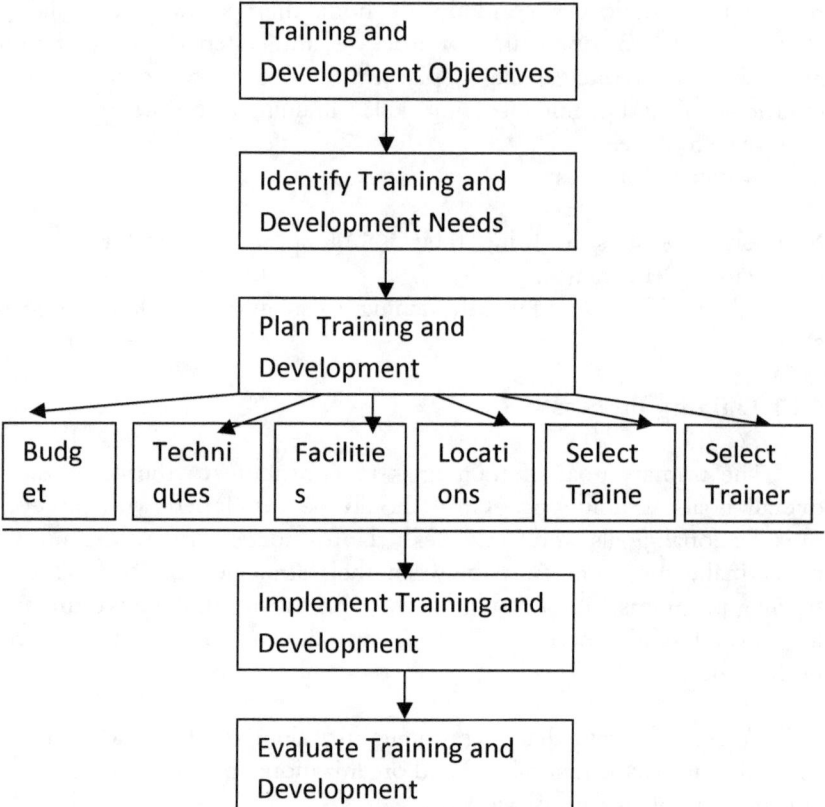

## Organization Analysis

Examination of the environment, strategies, and resources of the organization are to determine where training emphasis should be placed.

1. Economic and public policy issues.
2. Strategic initiative of an organization – Mergers and acquisition
3. Technological change, globalization, reengineering and TQM
4. Organizational restructuring, downsizing, empowerment and team work.

## Task Analysis

The second step in training-need assessment is task analysis. Task analysis involves reviewing the job description and specification to identify the activities performed in a particular job and the KSAs needed to perform them. The overall purpose is to determine the exact content of the training programme.

Steps
1. List all the tasks or duties included in the job
2. List the steps performed by the employee to complete each task.

## Person Analysis

Once the organization and task analysis have been made, it is necessary to perform a person analysis. Person analysis involves determining which employees require training and, equally important, which do not. Often performance appraisal information is used for person analysis.

Person Analysis is important for several reasons
- Helps organization avoid the mistake of sending of all employees into training.
- Helps managers determine what prospective trainees are able to do when they enter training so that the programs can be designed to emphasis the areas in which they are deficient.

## 4.2. Designing the training programme

Once the training needs have been determined, the next step is to design the type of learning environment necessary to enhance learning. Expect believes that training design should focus on at least four related issues:
1. Instructional objectives
2. Trainee readiness and motivation
3. Principles of learning
4. Characteristics of instructors

## Instructional Objectives

As a result of conducting organization, task, and person analyses, managers will have a more complete picture of training needs. On the basis of this information, they can more formally state the desired outcomes of training through written instructional objectives. Generally, instructional objectives describe the skills or knowledge to be acquired and/or the attitudes to be changed. One type of instructional objectives, the performance cantered objective, is widely used because it lends itself to an unbiased evaluation of results.

## Trainee Readiness and Motivation

Two preconditions for learning affect the success of those who are to receive training: readiness and motivation. Trainee readiness refers to both maturity and experience factors in the trainee's background. Perspective trainees should be screened to determine that they have the background knowledge and the skills necessary to absorb what will be presented to them.

The other precondition for learning is trainee motivation. For optimum learning to take place, trainees must recognize the need for new knowledge or skills, and they must maintain a desire to learn as training progress.

Managers can create a training environment that is conducive to learning. Six strategies can be essential.
1.  Use positive reinforcement
2.  Eliminate threats and punishment
3.  Be flexible
4.  Have participants set personal goals
5.  Designing interesting instruction
6.  Breakdown physical and psychological obstacles to learning

## Principles of Learning

Training has to build a bridge between employees and the organization. One important step in this transition is giving full consideration to the psychological principles or learning, that is, the characteristics of training programs that help employees grasp new material, make sense of it in their own lives, and transfer it back to the job. Because the success or failure of a training programme is frequently related to certain principles of learning, managers as well as employees should understand that different training methods or techniques vary in the extent to which they utilize these principles. Overall, training programmes are likely to be more effective if they incorporate the following principles of learning.

## Characteristics of Instructors

The success of any training effort will depend in large on the teaching skills and personal characteristics of those responsible for conducting the training. Training is influenced by the trainer's personal manner and characteristics. Here is some of desirable traits.

1.  Knowledge of subject
2.  Adaptability
3.  Sincerity
4.  Sense of humour
5.  Interest
6.  Clear instructions
7.  Individual Assistance
8.  Enthusiasm

## 4.2.1 Implementing the Training Program

A major consideration in choosing among various training methods is determining which ones are appropriate for the KSA s to be learned. In order to organize our discussion of various training methods, we will break them down into two primary groups.
1.  Training methods for non managerial employees
2.  Training methods for managerial employees

## Training methods for non managerial employees

A wide variety of methods are available for training employees at all levels. Some of the methods have a long history of usage. Newer methods have emerged over the years out of greater understanding of human behaviour, particularly in the areas of learning, motivation, and interpersonal relationships.

1.  On-the job training (OJT)
    This is method by which employees are giving hands-on experience with instructions from their supervisor or other trainers.
Drawbacks
a)  The lack of well structures training environment
b)  Poor training skills of managers
c)  The absence of well-defined job performance criteria
2.  Apprenticeship training
    System of training in which a worker entering the skill trades is given through instruction and experience, both on and off the job, in the practical and theoretical aspects of the work.
3.  Internship Programmes
    Programs jointly sponsored by campuses, universities, and other organizations that offer students the opportunity to gain real-life experience while allowing them to find out how they will perform in work organizations.

4. Classroom Instruction/training

Classroom training enables the maximum number of trainees to be handled by the minimum number of instructors. This method lends itself particularly to training in areas where information can be presented in lectures, demonstrations, films, and videotapes or through computer instruction.

5. Computer – Based Training (CBT)

As development of technology proceeds at a rapid place and the cost of computers continues to decline, high-technology training methods are finding increased use in industry, academia, and the military. Computer based training encompasses two distinct techniques: computer assisted instruction and computer managed instruction. Internet instruction: recently, organizations have begun exploring the internet as a potential vehicle for CBT.

6. Simulation Method

Sometimes it is either impractical or unwise to train employees on the actual equipment used on the job. An obvious example is training employees to operate aircraft, spacecraft, and other highly technical and expensive equipment. The simulation method emphasizes realism in equipment and its operation at minimum cost and maximum safety.

## Training methods for managerial employees

While many of the methods used to train first-level employees are also used to train manager and supervisors, other methods tend to be reserved for management development. Management development is instrumental for giving managers the skills and perspectives they need to be successful.

1. On the –job experience

Some skills and knowledge can be acquired just by listening and observing or by reading. But others must be acquired through actual practice and experience. By presenting managers with the opportunities to perform under pressure and to learn from their mistakes, on the job development experiences are some of the most powerful and commonly used techniques.

*Methods of providing on-the-job experiences include the following.*
a)  Coaching involves a continuing flow of instructions, comments, and suggestions from the manager to the subordinate.
b)  Understanding Assignments groom an individual to take over a manager's job by gaining experience in handling important functions of the job.

c)   Job Rotation provides, through a variety work experience, the broadened knowledge and understanding required to manage more effectively.

d)   Lateral Transfer involves horizontal movement through different departments along with upward movement in the organization.

e)   Special Projects provide an opportunity for individuals to become involved in the study of current organizational problems and decision-making activities.

f)   Action Learning gives managers release time to work full time on projects with others in the organization.

g)   Staff Meeting enables participants to become more familiar with problems and events occurring outside their immediate area by exposing them to the ideas and thinking of other managers.

h)   Planned career progression utilize all these different methods to provide employees with the training and development necessary to progress through a series of jobs requiring higher levels of knowledge and skills.

2. Seminars and Conferences

Seminars and conferences, like classroom instruction, are useful for bringing groups of people together for training and development. In management development, seminars and conferences can be used to communicate ideas, policies, or procedures, but they are also good for raising points of debate or discussing issues (usually with the help of a qualified leader) that have no set answers or resolutions. In this regard, seminars and conferences are often used when attitudes change is a goal.

3. Case Studies

A particularly useful method used in classroom learning situations is the case study.   Using documented examples, which may have been developed from the actual experience of participants in their own organizations, managers learn how to analyze (take apart) and synthesize (put together) facts, to become conscious of the many variables on which management decisions are based, and in general to improve their decision making skills.

4. Management Games

Training experiences have been brought to life and made more interesting through the development of management games, where players are faced with the task of making a series of decision affecting a hypothetical organization. The effects that every decision has on each area within the organization can be simulated with a computer programmed for the game. A major advantage of this technique is the high degree of participation it requires.

5. Role Playing

Role-playing consists of assuming the attitudes and behaviour-that is, playing the role-of others, often a supervisor and a subordinate who are involved in a particular problem. By acting out another's position, participants in the role-playing should also help them to learn how to counsel others by helping them see situations from a different point of view. It is used widely in training managers to handle employee issues relating to absenteeism, performance appraisal, and conflict situations.

## 4.2.2 Evaluating the training programme

Training, like any other HRM function, should be evaluated to determine its effectiveness. A variety of methods are available to assess the extent to which training programs improve learning, affect behaviour on the job, and impact the bottom-line performance of an organization.

There are four basic criteria available to evaluate training:
1. Reactions
2. Learning
3. Behaviour
4. Results

1: Reactions

One of the simplest and most common approaches to training evaluation is assessing participant reactions. Happy trainees will be more likely to want focus on training principles and to utilize the information on the job. However, participants can do more than tell you whether they liked a program or not. They can give insights into the content and techniques they found most useful.

2: Learning

Beyond what participants think about the training, it might be a good idea to see whether or not they actually learned anything. Testing knowledge and skills before a training program gives a baseline standard on trainees that can be measured again after training to determine improvement. However, in addition to testing trainees before and after training, parallel standards can be measured for individuals in a control group to compare with those in training to make certain that improvements are due to training and not some other factor.

3: Behaviour

This evaluates the extent to which behaviour has changed as required when people attending the programme have returned to their jobs. Trainees may not demonstrate behaviour change back on the job. Transfer of training refers to the effective application of principles learned to what is required on the job.

4: Results

According to an American Society of Training and Development (ASTD) study, approximately two-thirds of training managers surveyed reported that they were coming under additional pressure to show that their programs produce 'bottom line" results. Some of the results-based criteria used in evaluating training include increased productivity, fewer employee complaints, decreased costs and waste, and profitability.

## Benefits of effective training

Human Resources activities are more recognized and vital in performing the organizational activities due to the change of socio economic and socio cultural conditions in the globalized markets. Therefore, HR leaders and line leaders have to become allies for the economic value creation and the value improvement of the human assets. In other words, value oriented Human Resource management. Towards this objective planned HR training will have to give much contribution. Now, more and more emphasis is put on the knowledge economy and human capital.

Then planned training can minimize learning costs and increase organizational productivity in terms of quality, output, speed and performance. It also can improve operating flexibility through multi-skills, obtaining high level commitment from employees who are trained. Developing a positive culture within the organization also should be done. This can be done by providing people with the skills they need.

The training attracts high quality employees by offering them learning and development opportunities, increasing their levels of competence and enhances their skills, thus enabling them to obtain more job satisfaction; Help to manage change by increasing understanding of the reasons for change and providing people with the knowledge and skills they need to adjust to new situations; After training, employees should be reinforced which leads to give back the high level of customer service from satisfied internal customers.

## 4.3 Career Development

We may define career as the "occupational positions a persons has had over many years". Many people look back on they careers with satisfaction, knowing that what they might have achieved they did achieve, and that they career goals were satisfied. (Desseler 2007)

"A career is a series of work-related positions, paid or unpaid, that help a person grow in job skills, success and fulfilment". (Hutcheson, 1992)

Careers were traditionally viewed as an upward, linear progression in one or two firms or as stable employment within a profession. Today, some one's career is more likely to be driven by the person, not the organization and reinvented by the person from time to time as the person and environment change. Tomorrow's career won't be a same as today.

Armstrong (2006) has defined career management as one that "consists of the processes of career planning and management succession. Management succession planning takes place to ensure that, as far as possible, the organization has the managers it requires to meet future business needs.

We can define career management as a process for enabling employees to better understand and develop their career skills and interests, and to use this skills and interests most effectively both within the company and after they leave the firm.

A career is not only viewed from the perspective of the employee, as it normally understood. It is very much applicable to the organization's perspective as well. This is why management succession has come in to the picture. As you can see in the above definition, career management addresses such a perspective directly. Career management, therefore, refers to the effective and efficient use of employees to fill the vacancies that are likely to arise in the organization.

Today, the psychological contract between employers and employees has changed. Yesterday, employees traded loyalty for job security. Today, employees exchange performance for the sort of training and learning and development that will allow them to remain marketable.

### Importance of career management

Armstrong is of the view that career management has three major objectives: They are:
a) Satisfaction of organization's need for management succession
b) Paving way for promising employees to reach fullest work potential through training and experience, so that they can accept higher responsibility

c)  Providing necessary guidance and encouragement with a view to enabling promising employees achieve a successful career with the organization, in tune with their talents and aspirations.

Thus, career management has far reaching implications to the future of an organization. As you can see, there are cases of organizations having to bear the consequences of ineffective succession planning. The transition lacks smoothness and the efforts of a new leader or manager can appear to be abrupt.

## 4.3.1 Career management process

Every job has a career management process. A career management process identifies the step-by-step stages through which career progression takes place. Identifying such a process cannot be done in isolation. There are two tools are commonly used for this purpose: They are career dynamics and career analysis.

### Career dynamics

"Career dynamics describes how career progression takes place – the ways in which people move through their careers either upwards through promotion or by enlarging or enriching their roles to take on greater responsibilities or make more use of their skills and capacities" (Armstrong, 2006).

Career dynamics can help an organization formulate policies relating to career management. Such policies, in turn, help formulate management succession plans. Career dynamics is a study that is carried out by analyzing how the individuals progressed within the organization. This analysis is done function by function using information relating to performance appraisal. A trend line can be mapped out to identify variations from the actual data relating to employees. So what happens if there is a huge variation? The organization has to address this by making alterations to the career path. Faulty decisions in career dynamics and analysis can lead to over-promotion or stagnation of some employees as the policy can be prohibitive to move upwards in the organization.

### Career analysis

"Career analysis examines the characteristics of job ladders and families" (Armstrong, 2006).

What is a job ladder? As the name itself implies, it "consists of the steps individuals take as they progress through their career in a job family". A Job family consists of jobs where the nature of the work is essentially the same although there may be significant differences in the level of work undertaken". (Armstrong, 2006)  Career analysis also helps formulate policies for career management.  The organization can make a job ladder 'wide' enough to accommodate a wide variety of jobs so that there could be a uniform mode for progression.  If such 'widening' is impossible, the organization may have to develop parallel ladders.

## Career management policies

Career management policies spell out general guidelines for organizations to follow in decisions relating to meeting the HR needs in a given context.  Policies are framed to help managers follow a careful and well-considered approach and not make ad hoc haphazard decisions. Employees are also aware of what the organization's expectations are in terms of career management.  Thus, it is a 'two-pronged' approach where both the employer and employee are equal partners to it.  Let us now look at some career management policies Armstrong (2006):

## Make or buy decisions

This career management policy refers to the guiding principle that helps HR managers advocate an approach that either requires promotion of internal candidates or recruitment from external sources. For example, if an organization is of the view that it will fill 70% of senior position vacancies with internal promotions and 30% from external sources, it is a 'make or buy' decision.

Why might an organization have this approach? Either it can promote internal candidates or encourage new thinking entirely externally or it can have a mix of both.  Either way, such a policy is helpful when there is likely to be a shortage of a particular kind of human resource in the organization.

### Short- and long-term policies

Short-term policies reflect on managers taking a position where the best and most suitable employees are recruited for the current position. Such employees are provided with good terms and conditions in the organization, and based on their performance, they will be promoted to higher positions, when the 'time' comes.  In this approach, HR managers do not consider the long-term future to influence their decisions today. They are indeed concerned about the 'right here' and 'right now' issues. They consider that long-term issues would fall in to place.

### Long-term policies

In contrast to short-term policies, long-term policies look beyond a considerable time horizon.  Such a policy will adopt a rather structured approach towards career management because in this case, the organization would like employers to have a long-term view of their careers. As a result, performance appraisals and assessment centres are set up to verify and determine the extent to which the candidates have the necessary potential for such 'long-term' positions.

*Flexibility policies*

This approach is a more rational way of looking at career management. While the short-term is somewhat short-sighted and the long-term policy is rigid, this approach aims to adopt training and job rotation to act as a means to redirect career paths.

How does this policy, based on timeframes, work then? The short-term policies are most likely to be found in relatively small organizations and the long-term approaches in the more routine, bureaucratic ones, where a career is predictable. The flexibility approach is adopted by those organizations that do not fit in to neither small nor large ones.

## Specialist or generalists

This career management policy is for organizations that can have specialists and generalists in its rank and file. The organization may want to lay down an approach towards the career needs of its specialists – perhaps using a short-term approach. Similarly, it may develop an approach for generalists to move to management positions. Therefore, in such a context, dual career structures and career ladders may have to be adopted to help specialists, to either continue in their specialty or move over to a more generalist area. As you can see, such a policy is applicable for organizations that have large number of technical specialists.

## 4.3.2 Career planning

"Career planning shapes the progression of individuals within an organization in accordance with assessments of organizational needs and the performance, potential and preferences of individual members of the enterprise" (Armstrong 2006).

According to Dessler (2007), career planning and development is "the deliberate process through which a person becomes aware of personal career-related attributes and the lifelong series of stages that contribute to his or her career fulfilment".

"Career planning is the deliberate process through which someone becomes aware of personal skills, interests, knowledge, motivations, and other characteristics; acquires information about opportunities and choices; identifies career-related goals; and establishes action plans to attain specific goals" (Otte and Hutcheson, 1992).

*Importance of career planning*

a) It is a deliberate process: Career planning will not happen unless the individual is concerned about it and takes personal interest in it.

b) It shapes the career progression of individuals: Although career planning can have similarities across wide ranging jobs, it need not be identical to all individuals. Therefore, career planning can shape the progression of individuals.

c) It assesses organizational needs: Career planning is integrated to organizational needs. Although individuals make such plans, they are drawn up for individuals in accordance with what quality and quantity of human resource needs the organization requires for the given time and context.

d) It assesses performance, potential and preferences of individual: Career planning takes into account the full picture of the individual – performance, potential and preferences. It does not aim to be prescriptive and compel individuals to conform to what the organization requires.

e) It creates awareness of personal attributes contributing to career fulfilment: The first step of any plan is to know where one is and thereafter to look to where one wants to be. A career plan, therefore, helps create self-awareness.

f) It identifies career-related goals and establishes action plans to attain them: Probably the most important aspect of career planning is the identification of goals and action plans. As the questions in the previous section have illustrated, career plans lead to specific actions.

## 4.3.3 Career planning process

1. Identifying career stage

The first step in the career planning process is to identify the individual's career planning stage. Every individual has a career stage and the stage in which the individual is will influence one's preferences and interests for a career. Such a career stage is normally referred to as the 'career cycle'. "A career cycle is the stages through which a person's career evolves" (Dessler, 2007). The five stages are as follows:

*Growth Stage:*

The growth stage refers to the period from birth to age 14. During this stage, an individual forms the first impressions about his/her self-concept. One identifies him/herself with his/her immediate environment – family, friends, and school.

*Exploration Stage:*

This stage commences at age 15 and goes on till 24. During this stage, a more serious exploration of alternative occupations takes place. The once 'childish' and 'playful' role-plays begin to emerge as more concrete life-choices such as school education. The initial influences of school, leisure, interests and work begin to impress upon the future directions of the individual.

*Establishment Stage:*

This stage commences at 25 and goes on till 44. This stage is considered to be the 'heart' of people's work-lives. Several important events happen during this stage. It is assumed that the individual finds suitable initial employment. The individual engages in the employment activities with a view to seeking and achieving a permanent affiliation towards it.

*Maintenance Stage:*

During this stage, ranging from 45 to 65, individuals are more likely to move from stabilization to maintenance. The individual, in almost all cases, would have reached a significant position by this time in relation to his/her ambition in life. Thus, it would be more of maintenance of the position he/she has attained and achieved.

*Decline Stage:*

During this decline stage, the individual faces reduced powers, responsibilities and are more likely to be mentors and advisors to others who are coming up in earlier stages of their careers. Retirement is part and parcel of this stage.

2. Identifying occupational orientation

Another useful tool to identify one's career planning moves is through the identification of one's occupational orientation.

John Holland (1973) has suggested that an individual's values, motives and needs appear to be important determinants of that person's career choices. Accordingly, he developed six orientations:

a)  Realistic – involves occupations that require physical activities such as agriculture and farming
b)  Investigative – involves occupations that require organizing, imagining and thinking, such as a biologist or a professor
c)  Social – involves interpersonal skills such as social workers
d)  Conventional – involves structured, regulated activities such as accountants and bankers
e)  Enterprising – involves verbal activities that attract others such as lawyers, managers

f)    Artistic – involves creativity, expression and individual activities such as artists and musicians.

3. Identifying Skills:
Another step in the career planning process is the identification of occupational skills. Dessler (2007) has defined this concept as "the skills needed to be successful in a particular occupation". Similarly, aptitudes and special talents can also be identified for a career. Aptitudes are "innate abilities, which include intelligence, numerical aptitude, mechanical comprehension, and manual dexterity as well as talents such as artistic theatrical or musical ability that play an important role in career decisions" (Dessler, 2007).

4.Identify Career Anchors:
Career anchors were developed by Edgar Schein (1977). A career anchor is "a concern or value that you will not give up if a choice has to be made". What does an anchor do? It helps something else tied to it to remain steady. Anchors, in this context are pivots around which a person's career centres. Anchors may never be found in individuals unless and until they decide to make a major change in their work-lives. Schein identified five such anchors – technical; managerial competence; creativity; autonomy and independence; and security.

**Career planning techniques**
a)    Personal development planning
"Personal development planning is carried out by individuals with guidance, encouragement and help from their managers as required. A personal development plan sets out the actions people propose to take to learn and to develop themselves" (Armstrong 1999).
b)    Mentoring
"Mentoring is the process of using specially selected and trained individuals to provide guidance and advice which will help to develop the careers of the 'protégés' allocated to them" (Armstrong, 1999).
c)    Career counselling
Career counselling is the session that provides individuals the opportunity to discuss their aspirations and the employer the chance to comment on them – helpfully – and, at a later stage, to put forward specific career development proposals to be fed in to the overall career management programme (Armstrong 2006).

*****

# 5 PERFORMANCE MANAGEMENT

## 5.1 Introduction to Performance Management

Performance management is simply a term used to describe a set of activities that assess whether goals or objectives are being met. These activities include defining work, setting goals, providing feedback and encouraging development. Performance management is about shared responsibility and understanding of roles, expectations and standards.

Every day, we all ask ourselves: What do I need to do?, When shall I work on it?, How do I achieve the required quality?. These questions can apply to the day's work, or to the planning of the work for the next week, month or year. A manager's job is to decide whether an employee's achievements match what was expected. It is also.

The manager's task to connect the employee's work to organisational objectives. Your organisation may have formal performance management systems that require an annual appraisal or review. While these formal elements of performance management are important, the more critical.aspects of managing an individual's performance are daily interactions and feedback.

Performance that is not actively managed is nonetheless influenced by default. Failure to provide feedback means employees are unaware of whether their performance is acceptable and valued and can be a major disincentive to stay with the organisation. Furthermore, failure to manage negative performance can have harmful consequences on the morale of the rest of the work team.

## Basic concepts in Performance Review

A performance review is usually a structured meeting where an employee's performance over a given time period is assessed and future developmental needs are planned. The review should build on the informal performance management process that has been undertaken daily.. The main purpose is for both the manager and the employee to gain an overview, in the form of a retrospective summary of performance and a prospective look towards the employee's ongoing performance and development. The performance review is usually part of an organisational performance management system. It provides for consistency of practice across an organisation. Both feedback on, and development of performance are essential ingredients of managing performance. By fulfilling their duty to improve performance as par of their everyday work, managers increase the quality of employee work outputs and engagement...

Performance appraisal systems first began as simple methods of income justification. At this early stage appraisal was merely used to decide whether or not the salary or the wage of an individual employee was justified. The companies have some formal and informal means of appraising their employees' performance. Performance appraisal means evaluating an employee's current and past performance relative to his/her performance standards.

While the idea that appraisals should improve employee performance in nothing new, many managers take the integrated nature of that process of setting goals, training employees, and appraising and rewarding them more seriously today than they have in the past. These total integrated process call performance management. We may define performance management as a process that consolidates goal setting, performance appraisal, and development into a single, common system, the aim of which is to ensure that the employee's performance is supporting the company's strategic aims. ( Desseler 2007)

Performance appraisal may be defined as "the process of reviewing an individual's performance and progress in a job and assessing his potential for future promotion. It is a systematic method of obtaining, analysing and recording information about a person that is needed:

-   for the better running of the business ;
-   by the manager to help him to improve the job holders performance and plan his career;
-   by the job holder to assist him to evaluate his own performance and develop himself." (Amstrong, 2006).

A study (Oberg, 2004) identifies the goals of modern performance appraisal as to;

- help supervisors to observe their subordinates more closely and do a better coaching job,
- motivate employees by providing feedback on how they are doing,
- provide back-up data for management decisions concerning merit increases, transfers, dismissals etc.)
- improve organization development by identify people with promotion potential and pin-pointing development needs,
- establish a research and reference base for personnel decisions.

According to Amstrong (2006) there are three main groups of performance review activities:

1. Performance reviews - which relate to the need to improve the performance of individuals any thereby to improve the effectiveness of the organization as a whole.
2. Potential reviews - which attempt to deal with the problem of predicting the level and type of work that the individual will be capable of doing in the future.
3. Reward reviews - which relate to the distribution of such rewards as pay, power and status.

## 5.1.1 Performance Review Techniques

The purpose of a performance review is to analyse what a person has done and is doing in order to help him to do better. The phrase 'performance review' suggests a deliberate stock taking exercise. The most commonly used performance review techniques include:
Essay appraisal
Graphic rating scale
Forced - choice rating
Critical incident appraisal
Management - by - objectives approach
Ranking methods

Each of these techniques has its own strengths and weaknesses, and non is able to achieve all the purposes of performance review. The best managers can hope to do is to match an appropriate technique to a particular performance review goal.

*Essay Appraisal*

This technique requires the ratter to write a paragraph or more covering an individual's strengths, weaknesses, potential etc. In assessment situations involving professional, sales, or managerial positions, essay appraisal carry significant weight. The assumption being that an honest and informed statement either by word of mouth or in writing from someone who knows a person well is as valid as more formal methods. Essay ratings are difficult to combine or compare.

*Graphic rating scale*

This technique may not yield the depth of an essay appraisal, but it is more consistent and reliable. A graphic scale assesses a person on the quality and quantity of his work and on a variety of other factors that may vary with the job but usually include traits like reliability, cooperation etc. The graphic scale, though heavily criticized, remains the most widely used rating method.

*Forced - Choice rating*

In the forced - choice rating method ratters are asked to choose from among groups of statements those which best fit the individual being rated and those which least fit him. The statements are then weighted or scored in the same way a psychological test is scored. People with high scores are, by definition, the better employees; those with low scores are the poorer ones. Since the ratter does not know what the scoring weights for each statement are, in theory at least, he cannot play favourites. He simply describes his people, and the personnel department staff applies the scoring weights to determine who gets the best rating.

*Critical Incident Appraisal*

The critical incident method is an attempt to overcome the fundamental defects of the other schemes by focusing attention on behaviour. It is based on the principle of defining jobs in terms of the typical behaviour of job holders. The method asks manager familiar with a job to record critical incidents of successful or less successful job behaviour. After a large number of such incidents have been collected, they are categorized to form an overall picture of the typical types of behaviour that indicate either effective or ineffective performance.

*Management- by- objectives (MBO)*

Management-by-objectives (MBO) methods of performance review are result oriented They embody the principles developed by McGregor and the management by objectives philosophy based on the writings of Peter Drucker. The aim of this approach is to relate assessments to a review of performance against specific targets and standards of performance agreed jointly by superior and subordinate. The advantages of this procedure are that;

- the subordinate is given the opportunity to make his own evaluation of the results he obtains. When he is discussing results and the action that produced those results he is actually appraising him- self and gaining insight on how he can improve his own methods and behaviour.
- the job of the manager shifts from that of criticizing the subordinate to that of helping him to develop his own performance;
- It is consistent with the belief that people work better when they have definite goals which they must meet in specified periods.
- The difficulty encountered in this method is that of defining realistic and specific targets and standards and it is still necessary reviewing performance to analyse why the result was a relative success or failure as well as measuring what the result was.

*Potential Reviews*

Potential reviews are concerned with forecasting the direction in which an individual's career should go and the rate at which he is expected to develop. It provides information to the company on which it can base management succession plans and to the individual on his future with the company which may encourage him to stay and to improve his abilities further.

The assessment of potential requires the analysis of existing skills, qualities and how they can be developed to the mutual advantage of the company and the employee. It also requires the identification of any weaknesses which must be overcome if the employees full potential to be archived. Potential review also contains an important counselling aspect involving discussions with the individual about his aspirations and how these can best be matched to the future mapped out for him. These discussions are a vital part of the potential review procedure because they can provide the manager with information about his employee's feeling on this subject, which may have a marked effect on plans for development, including training and job rotation.

*Reward reviews*

In any company where rewards such as salary increments or bonuses are related to performance there has to be some method of linking the two together.

It is not advisable however, to have a direct link between the performance reviews and the reward reviews. Performance reviews must aim primarily at improving performance and assessing potential. If this is confused with a salary review, employees become over concerned about the impact of the assessment on the increment. Managers might give false assessment to ensure that their favoured staff gets the increments. Subordinates worry more about how much money is coming out of the process than about what they must do to improve performance for a more doubtful long term reward. It is better to separate the two processes thereby ensuring that the counselling and guidance can be carried out without everyone looking over their shoulders at their cash implications.

## 5.2. Performance appraisal procedures

Performance appraisal procedures should be based on the results oriented approach, as long as this allows for a review of why the result was archived as a basis for agreeing what needs to be done in the future.
The procedure should be as simple as possible- the use of a multiplicity of elaborate forms should be avoided.

The procedure should require managers to see their subordinates to discuss and agree targets and standards, to review performance, and to provide guidance and encouragement which will enable the individual to take action himself to develop his strengths or overcome his weaknesses.
The procedure should ensure that all concerned are properly briefed and trained.

Finally, provision must be made for assessments to be reviewed by the assessor's own superior, so that the individual being appraised does not feel he is at the mercy of a prejudiced boss. It may also be desirable to allow for formal appeals against assessments.

## 5.2.1 How to manage performance

*Factors affecting assessments:*
Assessments require the ability to judge people. Good judgement is a matter of fixing standards, considering only relevant evidence, avoiding projection and combining probabilities in their correct weight. The factors affecting assessment are those arising from;
-   The characteristics of the manager, including his ability to judge people, and his attitudes to the process of assessment;
-   The interaction between the manager and the interviewee;
-   The way in which the person being assessed is regarded by the manager - stereotyping.
-   The methods used to measure performance.

*Characteristics of the Manager:*

Most managers think they are good judges.  It is seldom that we meet any manager who admits to being a poor judge of people.  But mistakes made in selection, placement and promotion indicate that some managers are worse than others in judging people. Differences in personality characteristics will affect the type of judgements made and also the consistency and fairness of the judgements.  As a result, the attitudes of managers to their staff will vary so that different managers will appraise the same people quite differently.

It has also been discovered that if two managers are asked to rate the same people, not only do they rate against different standards, but the spread or scatter of their individual ratings will vary.  For example, one manager may produce ratings that group fairly closely around the person been judged, where as another managers ratings will be much more widely scattered.  The well-known 'halo effect' or its opposite, the 'horns effect' are associated with this speed factor.

Knowledge of these factors that affect assessment has strongly influenced the design of various performance review systems.  In an attempt to ensure consistency in judgements assessment characteristics have been defined and scales have been drawn up against which the ratings are made.  Elaborate statistical devices have been developed to eliminate variations.

However these systems have failed universally and the emphasis has returned to improving managers' skills in judging by;
-   Encouraging them to define standards and measures of effectiveness before hand and agree with those concerned.
-   Encouraging and training managers to avoid jumping to conclusion too quickly.
-   Providing manager with practice in judging people which enable them to identify their own weaknesses and improve themselves.

## Interaction between the manager and the interviewee:

Assessments are made by observation and discussion during interviews.  But their validity is affected by the following problems.
- Poor perception:- not noticing things or events for what they are;
- Wishful thinking:- noticing only those things one wants to see;
- Poor interpretation:- putting one's own interpretation on information;
- Projection:-  Seeing one's own faults in other people;

Empathy is required to obtain an accurate interpretation of a person's behaviour.  Empathy is the ability to put one self into someone else's shoes when trying to understand why he or she is behaving in a certain way.

The development of an effective performance review system is more a matter of overcoming the problems of making assessment and of improving empathy than of introducing elaborate procedures, whether they are traditional merit rating schemes or modern MBO programmes. There is a limit to which empathy can be induced- it is a skill and an attitude which managers have to develop for themselves.

Performance appraisal is a skilled process which, unfortunately, many managers are not very good at. Training is necessary to develop the skills required and to encourage an attitude of mind which ensures that managers will give this important aspect of their duties the emphasis it deserves.

## Managers' resistance to assessment

Appraisal programs tend to run into resistance from the managers who are expected to administer them. Even managers who admit the necessity of appraisal programs frequently resist the process especially the interview part. As a result some companies do not communicate appraisal results to employees, despite the general acceptance that the subordinate has a right to know his superiors opinion so that he can correct his weaknesses.

Manager's resistance is usually attributed to the following causes:
- Lack of skills needed to handle the interview.
- Dislike of a new procedure with its accompanying changes in way of operating.
- Mistrust of the validity of the appraisal instrument.

A formal control system, including scheduling, reminders etc are introduced in an attempt to overcome this problem of resistance. But even controls do not necessarily work. In certain instances even when there are signed documents by both the superior and the subordinate as evidence of appraisal interview been held, the subordinates when asked whether they have been told about their appraisal results have answered in the negative.

Training programs designed to teach skills of appraising and interviewing do help, but even such strategies seldom eliminate managerial resistance entirely. The difficulties connected with 'negative appraisals' remain a source of genuine concern. There is always some discomfort involved in telling a subordinate he is not doing well.

**The underlying cause:**

Perhaps this intuitive managerial reaction to conventional performance plans shows a deep but unrecognized wisdom. It does not reflect any thing as simple as resistance to change, or dislike for personnel techniques, or lack of skill, or mistrust for rating scales. Rather, managers seem to be expressing real misgiving, which they find difficult to put into words. This could be the underlying cause:

The conventional approach, unless handled with consummate skill and delicacy, constitute something dangerously close to a violation of the integrity of the personality. The respect we hold for the inherent value of the individual leaves us distressed when we must take responsibility for judging the personal worth of a fellow man. Yet the conventional approach to performance appraisal forces us not only to make such judgements and to see them acted upon but also to communicate them to those we have judged.

On this interpretation, then, resistance to conventional appraisal programs is eminently sound. It reflects an unwillingness to treat human beings like physical objects. The needs of the organization are obviously important, but when they come into conflict with our convictions about the worth and the dignity of the human personality one or the other must give.

## 5.3. Introduction of Job Evaluation

Job evaluation is of fundamental importance in reward management. It provides the basis for achieving equitable pay and is essential as a means of dealing with equal pay for work of equal value issues. In addition to relating pay levels to those paid for comparable jobs in other enterprises, the enterprise must also determine pay structures for its employees having different jobs within the organization. Factors similar to those affecting pay levels affect these pay structures too.

Managers can cope with the attempt to provide equal pay for positions of approximately equal worth by arbitrary management decisions, collective bargaining, or job evaluation. If managers try to make these decisions without help from tools such as job evaluation, it can result in unsystematic decision-making that is likely to lead to perceived inequities. Decisions based on bargaining alone can lead to outcomes based solely on relative power. Therefore, most management experts suggest that compensation decisions be based on systematic job evaluation, influenced by the results of collective bargaining. Later on in this course, you will be discussing collective bargaining; let us now discuss job evaluation.

Job evaluation is the formal process by which the relative worth of various jobs in the organisation is determined for pay purposes.

Essentially, it attempts to relate the amount of the employee's pay to the extent that her or his job contributes to organisational effectiveness (Glueck, 1978).

Desseler (2008) says Job evaluation is aimed at determining a job's relative worth. It is a formal and systematic comparison of jobs to determine the worth of one job relative to another and eventually results in a wage or salary hierarchy. The basic principle is: jobs that require greater qualifications, more responsibilities and more complex job duties should be paid at a highly level than jobs with lesser these requirements.

You will not find it easy to evaluate the worth of all the jobs in an enterprise. Take the example of a physician and a nurse's aid. It may be obvious that the effective physician will contribute more to the goals of patient care in the hospital than the nurse's aide; what is important is how much the differential is worth. Since it is difficult to compute how much a particular job contributes to organisational effectiveness, proxies for effectiveness are used.

Let us see what these proxies are. These are skills required to do the job, amount and significance of responsibility involved, effort required, and working conditions. Compensation must be in keeping with the differing demands of various jobs if employees are to be satisfied and if the organisation is to be able to attract the personnel it wants.

You should also know how job evaluation is done. It is usually performed by analyzing job descriptions and occasionally job specifications. Early in the process, it is imperative that job evaluator check the availability and accuracy of the job descriptions and specifications. It is usually suggested that job descriptions be split into several job series, such as managerial, professional, and technical, clerical and operative.

The next step is to select and weight the criteria used to evaluate the job. Typical factors frequently used for job evaluation are education, experience, amount of responsibility, job knowledge, and work hazards and working conditions. It is however important that the factors used are accepted as valid for the job by those being evaluated.

Once the method of evaluating the job is chosen, evaluators make job evaluations. As those familiar with the jobs tend to rate them higher, especially if they supervise the jobs, it is useful for each committee member to evaluate each job individually. Then the evaluators should discuss each job on which the ratings differ significantly, factor by factor, until agreement is reached.

## Approaches of Job Evaluation

There are two basic approaches to compare several jobs. First, we can take intuitive approach, we might decide that one job is more important than other and not dig any deeper into why. Second, as an alternative, we could compare the jobs by focusing on certain basic factors the jobs have in common. These call as compensable factors.

Some employers develop their own compensable factors, however most use factors popularized by packaged job evaluation systems or by federal legislation. For example, the equal pay act focuses on four compensable factors; skills, effort, responsibility and working conditions. The method popularized by the Hay Consulting Firm focused on three factors; know how, problem solving and accountability. Al-Mart bases its wage structure on knowledge, problem solving skill and accountability requirements.

Identifying compensable factors plays a central role in job evaluation. The compensable factors use depend on the job and the job evaluation methods, for example we might choose to include decision making for a manager' job, though it might be inappropriate for a cleaner' job. Job evaluation can be analytical or non-analytical; Jobs can also be valued by reference to their market rates.

*Analytical Job Evaluation:*

Analytical job evaluation is the process of making decisions about the value or size of jobs, which are based on an analysis of the level at which various defined factor or elements are present in a job in order to establish relative job value. Analytical job evaluation is the most common approach to job evaluation. The two main types of analytical job evaluation schemes are point factor schemes and factor comparison.

The main features of analytical job evaluation are that it is systematic, judgemental, concerned with person not the job, and deal only with internal relativities.

*Non-Analytical Job Evaluation:*

Non-Analytical job evaluation compares whole jobs to place them in a grade or rank order. They are not analysed by reference to their elements or factors. Non- analytical schemes do not meet the requirements of equal value. The main non-analytical schemes are Job classification and Job ranking.

## Preparation of Job Evaluation

Job evaluation is a judgemental process and demand close cooperation among supervisors, HR specialists and employees and union representatives. The main steps include identifying the need for program, getting cooperation, and choosing an evaluation committee. The committee than performs the actual evaluation.

Identifying the need for job evaluation should not be difficult. For example, dissatisfaction reflected in high turnover, work stoppages or arguments may result from paying employees different rates for similar jobs. Managers may express uneasiness with an informal way of assigning pay rates, accurately sensing that a more systematic assignment would be more equitable.

Getting employee to cooperate in the job evaluation is important. The job evaluation will provide a mechanism for considering the complaints they have been expressing; and that no present employee's rate will be adversely affected as a results of the job evaluation.

Choose a job evaluation committee. There are two reasons for doing so. First, the committee should include several people who are familiar with the job in question, each of whom may have a different perspective regarding the nature of the jobs. Second, if the committee is composed at least partly of employees, the committee approach can help ensure greater employee acceptance of the job evaluation results.

Therefore, the composition of the committee is important. The group usually consists of about five members, most of whom are employees. Management has the right to serve on such committees, but employee may view this with suspicion. However, a human resource specialist can usually be justified on the grounds that he or she has a more impartial outlook than line managers and can provide expert assistance.

## 5.3.1 Types of Job Evaluation

The four most frequently used job evaluation methods are:
1. Point factor Scheme
2. Factor comparison
3. Job Classification
4. Job Ranking

Although there is little research in the area, it appears that the four methods do about equally reliable jobs of evaluation.

*The Point Factor Scheme*
Most job evaluation plans use the point system, not only because it is more sophisticated than ranking and classification systems but also because it is relatively easy to use.

Essentially, the point system requires evaluators to quantify the value of the elements of a job. On the basis of the job description or interviews with job occupants, points are assigned to the degree of various factors for example, skill required, physical and mental effort needed, degree of dangerous or unpleasant working conditions involved, and amount of responsibility involved in the job. When these are summed, the job has been evaluated. Most point systems evaluate about ten aspects of each job. The aspects chosen should not overlap, should distinguish real differences between jobs, should be as objectively defined as possible, and should be understood and acceptable to both management and employees. Because not all aspects are of equal importance in all jobs, different weights reflecting the differential importance of these aspects to a job must be set. These weights are assigned by summing the judgments of several independent but knowledgeable evaluators. Thus a clerical job might result in the following weightings: education required 20 percent; experience required 25 percent; complexity of job, 35 percent; responsibility for relationships with others, 15 percent; working conditions and physical requirements, 5 per cent.

*Factor Comparison*

At the other extreme is the most complex system: the factor comparison method. This is probably the most costly, and it is probably slightly more reliable than the other methods.

The factor comparison method is actually a refinement of the ranking method. With the ranking method, you generally look at each job as an entity and rank the jobs on some overall factor like job difficulty. The factor comparison method requires five steps.

1. Choose the key jobs to be evaluated. These jobs are well known in the enterprise and, in the opinion of the evaluators, are properly paid, at present.
2. Rank the key jobs on important factors of job evaluation. These factors usually are mental requirements, skill requirements, physical requirements, responsibility, and working conditions.
3. Divide up the current pay among the factors. Thus, the rater is asked: If the jobs pay Rs.200.00 per hour, how much of the Rs.200.00 is for mental requirements? And so on.
4. Reconcile the differences in rankings found in steps 1 and 2 by the committee members.
5. Place the key jobs on a scale for each factor. This becomes the basis for evaluating non-key jobs in the structure.

*Job Classification*

Job classification is a simple, widely used method in which raters categorize jobs into group; all jobs in each group are of roughly the same value for pay purposes.

This system used in many levels of governments groups a set of jobs into a grade or classification. Then these sets of jobs are ranked in levels of difficulty or sophistication.

The classification approach is more sophisticated than ranking but less so that the point system or factor comparison. It can work reasonably well if the classifications are well defined. It is the second most frequently used system.

The classification method has several advantages. The main one is that most employers usually end up grouping jobs into classes anyway, regardless of the evaluation method they use. They do this to avoid having to work with and price an unmanageable number of jobs. The disadvantages are that it is difficult to write the class or grade descriptions, and considerable judgment is required to apply them.

*Job Ranking*

The simplest system, used primarily in smaller, simpler organisations, is job ranking. Instead of analysing the full complexity of jobs by evaluating parts of jobs, the job ranking method has the evaluator rank order whole jobs, from the simplest to the most challenging. Because of problems you will see below, ranking is probably the least frequently used method of job evaluation.

The evaluator sorts the jobs into ranks, allowing for the possibility of ties. If the list of jobs is large, the paired-comparison method, whereby each job is compared to every other job being evaluated, can be used. The evaluator counts the number of times a particular job is ranked above another, and the one with the largest number of highest rankings is the highest ranked. There is no assurance that the ranking thus provided is composed of equal-interval ranks. The differential between the highest job and next highest may not be exactly the same as that between the lowest and next lowest. If the system is used in an enterprise with many jobs to be rated, it is clumsy to use, and the reliability of the ratings is not good.

There are several steps in the job ranking method:
- Obtain job information: job descriptions for each job are prepared, and the information they contain about the job's duties is usually the basis for ranking jobs.
- Select and group jobs: it is often not practical to make a single ranking for all jobs in an organization. The usual procedure is to rank jobs by department.

86

- Select compensable factors: It is common to use just one factor and to rank jobs based on the whole job.
- Rank jobs: rank the jobs according to their job describtion from lowest to highest. Some managers use an alternation ranking method for making the procedure more accurate.
- combine rating: usually, several raters rank the jobs independently, then the rating committee can simply average the rankings.

*****

# 6 COMPENSATION MANAGEMENT

## 6.1 Definition of Compensation Management

Employee compensation refers to all forms of pay or rewards going to employees and arising from their employment. It has two components, direct financial payments such as wages, salaries, incentives, commissions and bonuses, and indirect payments like paid insurance and vacations.

Compensation is part of a transaction between an employee and an employer that results in an employment contract. From the employee's side, pay is a necessity in life. Compensation received for work is one of the major reasons people seeks employment. Pay is the means by which they provide for their own and their family's needs.

The compensation that an organization provides may be based on either membership (job) or performance (skill). In the traditional system, employees are paid according to the job or membership that has no connection with the employee's or organization's performance. On the contrary, in the case of performance or skill based pay, employees are compensated with respect to their performance, abilities, and knowledge. In practice, performance may be a minor determinant of compensation though academic theories extend the view that performance-based compensation leads to high motivation of employees (Decenzo and Robbins, 1999). Compensation, once determined, should not remain the same for years. It should be reviewed and changed after a certain period through a proper pay survey. Compensation serves many functions. Sound compensation can attract, motivate, and retain the competent employees of an organization (Werther and Davis, 1996).

Compensation is one of the most important functions in the HR functions for the employer, as well. Compensation claims a large part of the cash flow in an enterprise. It may be the major method used by an enterprise to attract the employees needed to get the work done, as well as a means to motivate employees for more effective performance.

Compensation is the monetary reward paid by an enterprise for the work done by an employee. You should note that compensation or pay is only one way: the employee is rewarded for work. Work also provides benefits, promotions and status, intrinsic rewards of the job, and other rewards. The relative importance of pay to the other rewards varies with the employee.

The word "reward" can be used interchangeably with compensation, employee compensation as a form of pay or rewards going to employees and arising from their employment. (Desseler 2007)

"Reward management is about how people are rewarded in accordance with their value to an organization. It is concerned with both financial and non financial rewards and embraces the philosophies, strategies, policies, plans and processes used by organizations to develop and maintain reward systems."(Armstrong, 2006)

## Objectives of Compensation

The objective of a compensation system is to create a system of rewards that is equitable to the employer and employee alike, so that the employee is attracted to the work and motivated to do a good job for the employer. Glueck (1978) cites Thomas Patten who suggests that in compensation policy there are seven criteria for effectiveness. The compensation should be:

- Adequate: Minimum governmental, union, and managerial levels should be met.
- Equitable: Each person is paid fairly, in line with his or her effort, abilities, training, and so on.
- Balanced: Pay, benefits, and other rewards provide a reasonable total reward package.
- Cost effective: Pay is not excessive, considering what the enterprise can afford to pay.
- Secure: The employee's security needs relative to pay and the needs which pay satisfies are met
- Incentive providing: Pay motivates effective and productive work.
- Acceptable to the employee: The employee understands the pay system and feels it is a reasonable system for the enterprise and himself.

## 6.1.1 Compensation Decision Making

Three groups of managers are involved in compensation decisions. The first are HR executives; the HR department develops the pay system and administers it. For smaller enterprises, the HR specialist does this as part of the total job. When an enterprise has more than about 500 employees, a compensation manager may be made responsible for the compensation activity. The compensation administrator is a consultant, coordinator, catalyst, and implementer of the system, which is designed in conjunction with top managers and the chief HR executive.

Secondly, operating managers make the raise decisions, but a crucial factor is the policy decisions made by the third group, top management. They determine the pay policies of the enterprise. Top managers make the decisions that determine the total amount of the budget that goes to pay, the form pay will take and other pay policies such as raise levels, secrecy and communication policies, security in pay policies, and executive compensation. Compensation decisions, then, generally are made by operating management and administrated and implemented by HR.

Pay can be determined absolutely or relatively. There is a school of thought that a pay system set by a single criterion for a whole nation or the world, an absolute control of pays, is the best procedure. However, attempts to use this approach, was not a great success. Since absolute pay systems are not used, the pay for each individual is set relative to the pay of others.

Glueck (1978) cites Allen Nash and Stephen Carrol who point out that pay for a particular position is set relative to three groups. These are:
• Employees working on similar jobs in other enterprises (Group A).
• Employees working on different jobs within the enterprise (Group B).
• Employees working on the same job within the enterprise (Group C).

The decision to examine pay relative to group A is called the pay-level decision. Let us look at this first. The objective of the pay-level decision is to keep the enterprise competitive in the labour market. The major tool used in this decision is the pay survey. The pay decision relative to group B is called the pay-structure decision and uses job evaluation. The decision involving pay relative to group C is called individual pay-determination.

Arstrong (2006) says that there are five economic factors influencing pay levels such as labour market, supply and demand, efficiency wage theory, human capital theory, and agency theory.

Desseler (2007) has analysed four main determinants that can influence pay rates, and these are legal considerations, union influences, compensation policies and equity.

## 6.2 Methods of Payment

### Payment for Time Worked

Employees can be paid for the time they work, the output they produce, or a combination of these two factors. The great majority of employees are paid for time worked, in the form of wages or salaries. Pay surveys are used to establish competitive pay for the industry, and job evaluation is the principal method for setting time-pay schedules. Then pay ranges, pay classifications, and similar tools are developed for individual pay determination, the final step in a time-based pay system.

Typically, most employees are paid salaries; exceptions are blue-collar and some clerical employees, who are paid hourly wages. One issue in the time-pay system is whether everyone should be paid a salary. Would you rather be paid strictly by the hour and not know your income week to week, month to month, or be paid a salary so you could plan your life? In general, most blue-collar employees are given hourly pay, but there has been a movement to place all employees on salaries and give them the same benefits and working conditions others have.

The success of a total-salaries program requires stable, mature, responsible employees, a cooperative union, willing supervisors, and a work load that allows continuous employment.

### Incentive Plans

The methods for paying employees on the basis of output are usually referred to as incentive forms of compensation. Incentives can be paid individually, to the work group, or on an enterprise wide basis. Incentive compensation assumes it is possible and useful to tie performance directly to pay.

### *Individual Incentives*

The oldest form of compensation is the individual incentive plan, in which the employee is paid for units produced. Today, the individual incentive plan takes several forms: piecework, production bonus and commissions. These methods seek to achieve the incentive goal of compensation. One or more of these methods may be there in your workplace as well.

Straight piecework usually works like this: an employee is guaranteed an hourly rate for performing an expected minimum output. For production over the standard, the employer pays so much per piece produced. This is probably the most frequently used incentive pay plan. The standard is set through work measurement studies, as modified by collective bargaining. The base rate and piece rates may develop from pay surveys.

A variation of the straight piece rate is the differential piece rate. In this plan, the employer pays a smaller piece rate up to standard and then a higher piece rate above the standard. Experience shows that the differential piece rate is a more effective incentive than the straight piece rate, although it is much less frequently used.

Commissions are paid to sales employees. Straight commission is the equivalent of straight piecework and is typically a percentage of the price of the item. A variation of the production bonus system for sales is to pay the salesperson a small salary and commission or bonus when she or he exceeds standard.

Individual incentives are used more frequently in some industries than others and more in some jobs than others. For incentive schemes to work, they must be well designed and administered. It has been observed that incentive plans are likely to be more effective under certain circumstances. These are when:

- The task is liked.
- The task is not boring.
- The supervisor reinforces and supports the system.
- The plan is acceptable to employees and managers and probably includes them in plan design.
- The standards are carefully designed.
- The incentive is financially sufficient to induce increased output.
- Quality of work is not especially important.
- Most delays in work are under the employees' control.

## Group Incentives

Piecework, production bonuses, commissions and other individual incentives can also be paid to groups of individuals. This might be done when it is difficult to measure individual output, when cooperation is needed to get production, and when management feels this is a more appropriate unit on which to base incentives. Group incentive plans also reduce administrative costs. Group incentive plans are used less frequently than individual incentive plans.

## Enterprise Incentive Schemes

Four approaches to incentive plans are used at the enterprise level: suggestion systems; company group incentive plans; profit sharing; and stock ownership plans.

(a) Suggestion Systems

Most large and medium-size enterprises have suggestion systems designed to encourage employee input for improvements in enterprise effectiveness. Typically, the employee submits the suggestion in writing, perhaps placing it in a suggestion box. If, after being screened by a committee, the idea is tried and proven useful, the employee receives a financial reward. If the savings due to the idea are hard to compute, the employee is given a standard reward. If they are measurable, the employee receives a percentage of the first year's savings, typically 10 to 20 percent.

## (b) Company Group Incentive Plans

Several enterprises have developed elaborate group incentive and participation schemes, which generally have been quite successful. For these plans to succeed, management must be willing to encourage and work with participating workers. All workers must provide their fair shares of suggestions and work. The union must develop a new degree of cooperation. It is likely to be more successful in organisations that are less than gigantic. It also has worked well in troubled companies that provide the necessary conditions of participation, communication, and identification.

## (c) Profit Sharing Plans

Essentially, profit sharing is the payment of a regular share of company profits to employees as a supplement to their normal compensation. Many enterprises do this today. Profit sharing plans divide a set percentage of net profit among employees. The percentage varies, but 25 per cent is about normal. The funds can be divided equally based on the base salary or job grade, or in several other ways. The profit share can be paid often or less frequently, or deferred until retirement.

Advocates of profit sharing contend that the plans successfully motivate greater performance by employees. Many firms also see profit sharing as a way to increase employee satisfaction and quality workmanship and to reduce absenteeism and turnover. Essentially, they contend that employees who have profit-sharing plans identify more closely with the company and its profit goal, and thus they reduce waste and increase productivity.

## (d) Stock Ownership Plans

Many companies encourage employee purchase of company stock (often at advantageous prices), to increase employees' incentives to work, satisfaction, and work quality, and to reduce absenteeism and turnover. Purchase plans often allow for payroll deductions or company financing of the stock. Sometimes, the company will agree to buy the stock back at a guaranteed rate if it appears that the employee would take a significant loss. Companies use these plans for the same reasons as they do profit sharing plans: when employees become partners in the business, they work harder.

Some of these plans are very successful. But in general, stock purchase plans have most of the disadvantages of profit sharing. It is hard for an employee to identify his working harder with an increase in the value of his stock.

## 6.2.1 Trends in Compensation

### Competency based pay

Competency based pay is where the company pays for the employee's range, depth, and types of skills and knowledge, rather than for the job title. We can simply define competencies as demonstrable characteristics of the person, including knowledge, skills, and behaviours, that enable performance.

Why pay employees based on the skill, knowledge, or competency level they achieve rather than based on the duties of the jobs they are assigned. There are several good reasons:

- Traditional pay plans may actually backfire if a high performance work system is your goal.
- Paying for skills, knowledge and competencies is more strategic
- Measurable skills, knowledge, and competencies are the heart of any company's performance management process.

### Compensating the Managers and Professionals

One of the most controversial groups in terms of designing reward structures is the CEOs of large privately held firms. It is well known that they make many times as the average worker and according to Ivancevich (1998), especially in medium sized and small corporations, the ratio with the average worker is 15:1 or less. While the executive pay is of interest to stockholders, managers and other employers, the basis upon which it is built has been changing. Traditionally, executives' salaries were based on the competitive-pay approach. Companies within and across industries would act as if they were engaging in a price war, trying to outbid each other with fat pay envelopes for proven performers.

Today, executive pay packages are more likely to be based on comparative performance. This new pay design has five underlying principles (Ivancevich, 1998):

1. Compensation committees made up of stockholders and company directors link CEOs' pay to returns to shareholders.
2. Variable performance-based pay is emphasised over guarantees.
3. CEOs are encouraged to invest in company stock.

4.  Performance yardsticks are linked to actual key productivity indices, to the competition, or to both.
5.  CEOs are held responsible for the cost of capital; this forces them to look for vehicles of growth rather than just amass personal wealth.

## Executive Perks

In addition to the pay, executives receive special perquisites and extras commonly called perks. In different countries these may vary, but generally they include: better office decor; choice office location; a company car; reserved parking; a car for personal use; and first-class air tickets. In this block, the details are covered under the topic of employee benefits.

## Bonuses

A bonus is a compensation payment that supplements salary and can be paid in the present or in the future, in which case it is called a deferred bonus. The size of bonuses and long-term payments relative to salary clearly changes with the size of the chief executive officer's company. The larger the company, the greater is the proportion of incentive awards making up total annual compensation. A majority of large firms pay bonuses, on the belief that this leads to better profitability and other advantages for enterprises.

Determining compensation package for professional employees such as scientists, accounts, engineers, lawyers and doctors can be more complex because the job requires unique demand such as analysis and creativity. On the other hand, the impact of performance of such employee on the organization may only be indirect. Therefore, employers normally adopt the market pricing approach to determine pay rates for professional employees.

## 6.3 Employee Benefits and Services

Employee benefits and services are a part of the rewards including pay and promotion that reinforce loyal service to the employer. Major benefits and services programmes include pay for time not worked, subsidised insurance, subsidised retirement and services (Glueck, 1978). This definition is a bit vague because the term 'benefits and services' is applied to hundreds of programmes. This includes things like health and life insurance, pensions, time off with pay, and child care assistance.

Employee benefits include pensions, sick pay, insurance cover, company cars and a number of other "perks". They comprise elements of remuneration additional to the various forms of cash pay and also include provisions for employees that are not strictly remuneration, such as holidays. (Armstrong 2006)

The programmes offered in work organisations today are the product of efforts in this area for the past 30 years. Some employers provide these programmes for labour market reasons; that is, to keep the enterprise competitive in recruiting and retaining employees in relation to other employers. Or they may provide them to keep a union out, or because the unions have won them. Another reason often given is that they are provided because they increase employee performance.

International Labour Organization at its Asian Regional Conference 1950 defined labour welfare as a term which is understood to include…..
"such services, facilities, amenities as may be established in or in the vicinity of undertakings to enable the employees to perform their work in a healthy, congenial surroundings and to provide them with amenities conductive to good health and high morale"

The employee benefits and services is a concept that could be placed between; a) moral and ethical obligation of the employer, and b) earned right of the employee based on law and contract.

A formal definition is that employee benefits include any benefit or service that an employee receives in addition to his/her direct remuneration. The terms services and benefits are interchangeable, benefit are those for which monetary value can be ascertained, and services are those for which direct monetary value cannot be readily established.

## Objectives of employee benefits

The objectives of the employee benefits policies and practices of an organization are to:

- Provide an attractive and competitive total remuneration package which both attracts and retains high-quality employees.
- Provide for the personal needs of employees.
- Increase the commitment of employees to the organization.
- Provide for some people a tax-efficient method of remuneration.

These objectives do not include "to motivating employees". This is because the normal benefits provided by a business seldom make a direct and immediate impact on performance. They can, however create more favourable attitudes towards the business which can improve commitment and organizational performance in the longer term.

## 6.3.1 Important of the Fringe Benefits

Employee benefits and services are alternatively known as fringes. Fringes embrace a broad range of benefits and services that employee receive as a part of total compensation package. Benefits and services are indirect compensation extended as a condition of employment but not directly related to the performance. Beardwell and Holden (1998) list some of the reasons for using fringe benefits:

- Most fringe benefits do not attract tax and therefore can be advantageous for employer and employee, particularly the high earner.
- Some benefits can be provided cheaply through economies of scale.
- Some benefits are needed to facilitate the execution of the job duties of the employee: for example, company cars for sales representatives, and special equipment or clothing.
- Some companies may be able to offer discounts on their own products or services, for example, banks and building societies, retailers, car manufacturers, etc.

It should be remembered that most benefits are taxable as benefits in kind, the notable exceptions being approved pension schemes, meals where these are generally available to employees, car parking spaces, professional subscriptions and accommodation where this is used solely for performing the duties of the job.

## Flexible/Cafeteria Benefits

There appears to be a movement towards flexible compensation schemes more commonly known as 'cafeteria benefits.' (Beardwell and Holden, 1998). Cafeteria benefit schemes operate by setting a 'price' for each level of the selected benefits within a menu and each employee is allocated a budget to spend on benefits, expressed as credits, points or cash amounts. Thus employees are able to decide which benefits they prefer and how to balance the amount of cash pay to benefits.

Though companies have not adopted 'cafeteria benefits' on a large scale, Beardwell and Holden provide some of the objectives of those employers who do introduce flexible benefit schemes:

- to ensure flexibility in the compensation package to improve retention and recruitment.
- to offer employees the rewards they desire and thereby increase their motivation.
- to maintain 'value for money' with the benefits provided.
- to create single status employment.

Flexible benefit schemes allow employees to decide, within certain limits, on the make-up of their benefits package. Schemes can allow for a choice within or a choice between benefits. Employees are allocated an individual allowance to spend on benefits. This allowance can be used to switch between benefits, to choose new ones or to alter the rate of cover within existing benefits. Some core benefits such as sick pay may lie outside the scheme and cannot be flexed. Employees can shift the balance of their total reword package between pay and benefits, either adding to their benefits allowance by sacrificing salary or taking any unspent benefit allowance as cash. Flexible benefit schemes provide employees with a degree of choice on what benefits they want, according to their needs.

## 6.4. Types of Employee Benefits

There are many ways to classify the benefits and services. We will classify them as 1) legally required benefits, 2) contingent or deferred payment,3) payments for time not for work, 4) personal service benefits and 5) other benefits.

### Legally required benefits:

There are mainly three legally required benefits as health and safety, workman's compensation, and terminal benefits.

*Health and safety:*

Health and safety insurance looms large in many people's choice of employer, because such insurance is so expensive, most employers therefore offer some type of hospitalisation, medical, and disability insurance. This insurance helps protect employees against hospitalisation cost and the loss of income arising from off the job accidents or illness.

*Workman's compensation:*

The workman's compensation ordinance provides for payment of compensations by the employer to a workman who sustains personal injury in certain circumstances. There is no longer any distinction between adults and minor and the ordinance now applied to all employees. A "workman" is defined as any person who works under a contract with an employer for the purpose of his trade or business in any capacity whether the contract expressed or implied, oral r writing and whether it is a contract of service or apprenticeship or a contract personally to execute any work or labour.

*Terminal/Superannuary benefit:*

Employees' Provident Fund (EPF): The Employees' Provident Fund Act No.15 of 1958. They ensure retiring benefits to employed persons by means of a contributory provident fund and are based on the principle that superannuating of employees is the joint responsibility of the employee and employer

Employees' Trust Fund (ETF): ETF Act no.46 of 1980 established an employees' trust fund to which employers are required to contribute a percentage of the earnings of an employee. The current rate is 3%. No contributions can be made by an employee.

Gratuity: The Payment of Gratuity Act No.12 of 1983 provides for the payment of gratuity to employees employed in any plantation, trade, business or manufacturing industry covered by the Act.

## Contingent or deferred payment

Pension schemes: these are generally regarded as the most important employee benefit. Pensions plan are financial programs that provide income to individuals in their retirement.

Personal security; these are benefits which enhance the individual's personal and family security with regard to illness, health, accident or life insurance.

Severance pay: a onetime payment some employers provide when terminating an employee. Severance pay makes sense; it is a humanitarian gesture and good public relations.

## Payments for time not for work

### *Vacations and holidays:*

The number of paid employee vacation days varies considerably from employer to employer. In Sri Lanka, casual leave 7 days and annual leave 14 days per year. These will be on a non cumulative basis. Casual leave should not normally exceed 02 days at a time nor immediately precede nor follow annual leave. In your first year of employment you shall be entitled to one day's casual leave for each completed period of 02 months service. At least one stretch of annual leave shall be of not less than 07 days duration. As far as practicable you will be required to adhere to a roster prepared at the commencement of the year.

### *Sick leave:*

Sick leave provides pay to employees when they are out of work due to illness. Most sick leave policies grant full pay for a specified number of sick days. In Sri Lanka, usually up to 21 days per year. Sick leave exceeding 2 days at a time shall be supported be a certificate from a registered medical practitioner.

## Personal service benefits

Financial assistant: loans, house purchase schemes, relocation assistance and discounts on company goods or services.

Personal needs: entitlements which recognize the interface between work and domestic needs or responsibilities, examples holidays and other forms of leave, child care, career breaks, retirement counselling, financial counselling and personal counselling in times of crisis, fitness and recreational facilities.

## Other benefits

The main areas in which allowances and other special payments may be made to employees are:

*   Location allowance: Allowance are paid as an addition to basic salary although many employers in effect consolidate them by paying the local market rate which takes into account explicit or implicit location allowances and costs.
*   Subsistence allowance: the value of subsistence allowance for accommodation and meals varies greatly between organizations. Some have set rates depending on location or the grade of employee.
*   Overtime payments: most of manual workers are eligible for paid overtime as well as many staff employees up to management level. Higher paid staff may receive time off in lieu if they work longer hours.
*   Shift payments: are made at rates which usually vary according to the shift arrangement.
*   Stand-by and call-out allowance: may be made to those who have to be available to come in to work when required. The allowance may be made as a standard payment added to basic pay. Alternatively, special payments may be made for unforeseen call-outs.
*   Company cars and fuel: still much appreciated benefit in spite of the fact that cars are now more heavily taxed.
*   Other benefits: which improve the standard of living of employees such as subsidized meals, clothing allowances, refund of telephone costs, mobile phone and credit card facilities?
*   Intangible benefits: characteristics of the organization which contribute to the quality of working life and make it an attractive and worthwhile place in which to be employed.
*   Housing scheme: is a basic requirement and should be of concern, it is costly service and many employers provide technical support, provide loans or rent allowance.
*   Canteen service: is a desirable facility, some organization provide free meals or subsidized meals.
*   Medical scheme: is a primary need, there is a company medical officer in some organization, and some organizations are allowing reimbursing the medical bills.

Companies need to recognize what they want to achieve from the provision of each benefit and understand the motivational characteristics of each benefit for their own employees.

## 6.4.1 Management of benefits and services

Benefits and service are an integral part of effective human resources management. The management f employee service is very complex requiring considerable time and effort. In routine management operational and technical aspects are considered more important than strategic considerations. However strategic considerations are also vital. There are some of the strategic issues which should be taken cognisance of:

- How much of total compensation inclusive of benefits should be provided?
- What percentage should benefits consist of the total compensation?
- What are the objectives of offering each type of benefits?
- What is the expense level for each benefit?
- What categories of employees are entitled to which benefits?

## Basic principles of managing benefits and services:

- Benefits and services must be provided on the basis of a genuine interest in the protection and promotion of well being, not thrust upon the management a matter of charity and it should satisfy a real need.
- Benefits and services must be cost effective and broad based as possible.
- It should be preceded by sound planning with employee consideration.
- Employees should be educated to make use of the benefits.

*****

# 7 GRIEVANCE AND DISCIPLINE

## 7.1. Grievance Handling

The employees feel that there is no means of raising their concerns, and then these issues are unlikely ever to be resolved. There are a variety of likely outcomes, one of which is that employees become more and more discontented and ultimately may decide to leave. Therefore, for the sake of justice to the individual and smooth functioning of the whole organisation, it is important for the management to get at the root of employee dissatisfaction and to take corrective action wherever possible.

When someone expresses his dissatisfaction, you can then designate such action as a complaint. Usually, but not always, when a person 'sounds off' about something that bothers him, he hopes that the listener will do something to correct his difficulty. It is much more important for management to know about dissatisfaction. An unexpressed dissatisfaction is as worthy of consideration by the supervisor as the spoken complaint.

To understand what a grievance is, you must clearly be able to distinguish between dissatisfaction, complaint and grievance. Torrington (1987) provides us with a useful categorisation in this regard:

- Dissatisfaction: anything that disturbs an employee, whether or not the unrest is expressed in words.
- Complaint: a spoken or written dissatisfaction brought to the attention of the supervisor or the shop steward.
- Grievance: a complaint that has been formally presented to a management representative or to a union official.

In addition, there are other definitions of a grievance that distinguish it from the other two. Some such definitions are:

- A grievance is a formal dispute between an employee and management on the conditions of employment. (Glueck 1978)
- Grievances are complaints that have been formally registered in accordance with the grievance procedure. (Jackson, 2000)
- A grievance is any dissatisfaction or feeling of injustice in connection with one's employment situation that is brought to the attention of the management. (Beach 1980)

There are many reasons why employees keep their problems inside themselves. A person may simply have a high tolerance limit for frustration; feel that the condition may soon change in such a way that the problem will then be corrected; have found from past experience that it does not good to complain to his/her supervisor. Sometimes a person may even feel that others will criticise or condemn him if he complains.

Suppressing grievances would not be conducive to the smooth functioning of an organisation. Unheard and unattended grievances generally lead to unhappiness, frustration, discontentment, inefficiency and low productivity. Jackson (2001) refers to several potential outcomes when the employees feel that managers have failed to respond to their grievances or handled them badly:

From the standpoint of an employer, there is a correlation between grievance filing and higher absenteeism and fewer production hours. High grievance levels are also associated with a conflict labour relations climate (Heneman, 2000). Further, if employees feel that they have been badly treated, they are more likely to be resistant to proposed changes.

## 7.1.1 Types of Grievances

Grievances arise from various issues. Different authors take different approaches in describing the types of grievances. Heneman (2000) suggest the following categories to flag the most prevalent issues.

*Customs and Practice*

Many practices are not explicitly spelled out in the contract, but have grown up over time. For example, it may be customary to allow wash-up time at the end of the shift. If management changes procedures, a grievance may result. Practice, even though not spelled out, may take on the form of a contract clause, particularly if management has cited it as a reason not to grant other concessions during negotiations.

*Rule Violations*

Work rules are often spelled out in contracts or supplementary materials. When an employee violates one, he is subject to discipline. There may be a dispute regarding whether the violation occurred and if so, whether the discipline is excessive for the violation.

*Insubordination*

Violations of orders or refusal to perform assigned work are leads to insubordination charges. Generally, employees are expected to perform the required work and then grieve its assignment rather than refuse to do it. There may be instances, such as safety situations, where employees may rightfully refuse to perform the work under the contract.

*Absenteeism*

Excessive absenteeism is frequently a cause for discipline. Grievances generally occur where employees are not treated consistently or where the discipline is seen as being excessive for the level of absences.

*Dishonesty*

Cases of theft usually result in discharge. Most grievances here relate to searches and seizures and other alleged violations of evidentiary procedures.

*Substance Abuse*

Employees may be disciplined and/or discharged for drug use on company premises or where their performance is negatively influenced by prior acute or chronic use of intoxicants. Substance abuse is frequently involved with absence behaviour.

Thus, you will note that grievances arise for a variety of issues. However, the range of issues and types included within the scope of grievance procedures varies from one workplace to another.

## 7.1.2 Causes of Grievances

Nair and Nair (1999) refer to a US study and 2 Indian studies identifying typical grievances and common causes for the same. Despite differences in culture, industrial climate and per capita income levels between the US and India, the authors found that the findings were almost equally applicable to both countries.

The causes of grievances as arising from the following issues:
- working environment, e.g., light, space, heat
- use of equipment, e.g., tools that have not been properly maintained

- supervisory practices, e.g., workload allocation
- personality clashes and other inter-employee disputes (work-related or otherwise)
- behaviours exhibited by managers or other employees, e.g., allocation of 'perks' such as Sunday overtime working, and harassment, victimisation, and bullying incidents
- refused requests, e.g., annual leave, shift changes
- problems with pay: e.g., late bonus payments, adjustments to overtime pay
- perceived inequalities in treatment: e.g., claims for equal pay, appeals against performance related pay awards
  organisational change, e.g., the implementation of revised company policies or new working practices.

Following is a broad classification of grievances and their causes identified by the US Dept. of Labour, as quoted.

| Classification | Causes |
|---|---|
| 1. wage grievances | - demand for individual wage adjustment<br>- complaint about job classification<br>- complaint about incentive system<br>- miscellaneous |
| 2. supervision | - complaint against discipline/ administration<br>- complaint against behaviour of supervisor<br>- objection to the method of supervision |
| 3. working conditions | - safety and health<br>- violation of rules and regulations<br>- miscellaneous |
| 4. seniority promotion and transfers | - loss of seniority<br>- calculation/ interpretation of seniority<br>- promotion – denial or delay<br>- transfer or change of shifts |
| 5. discipline | - discharge/ dismissal/ layoffs<br>- alcoholism, absenteeism and accidents<br>- harshness of punishment and penalty |
| 6. collective bargaining | - violation of contract /award/ agreement<br>- interpretation of contract/award/ agreement<br>- settlement of grievances |
| 7. union management relations | - recognition of union<br>- harassment of union bearers<br>- soldiering / go-slow tactics |

## 7.2. The Grievances Handling Procedure

Grievance handling procedures involve a systematic set of steps for handling an employee complaint/grievance. Most union contracts provide the channels and mechanisms for processing these grievances.

Jackson (2000) lays down the objectives of a grievance handling procedure as follows:
- To enable the employee to air his/her grievance
- To clarify the nature of the grievance
- To investigate the reasons for dissatisfaction
- To obtain, where possible, a speedy resolution to the problem
- To take appropriate actions and ensure that promises are kept.
- To inform the employee of his or her right to take the grievance to the next stage of the procedure, in the event of an unsuccessful resolution

You will have by now realised that handling complaints and grievances in a fair and efficient manner in the workplace, can significantly contribute to good employee-employer relations. Admittedly, this can be achieved by good management practices alone, but it is generally preferable to adopt a formal written policy and procedure, to ensure consistency and a coordinated approach. Managers, who believe that it introduces unnecessary rigidity into the working relationship, however often resent the formality of the grievance handling procedure. Formality in procedure provides a framework within which individuals can reasonably air their grievances and avoid the likelihood of managers dodging the issue when it is difficult. It avoids the risk of inconsistent ad hoc decisions and the employee knows at the outset that the matter will be heard and where it will be heard.

Some employers, especially in non-union companies, take the view that there is really no need for establishing a formalised grievance handling procedure. Their view is that all their first line supervisors are trained to hear employee complaints and to take prompt action to settle them. They also state that the company is well managed, it has an enlightened human relations programme in operation, and employees generally are well satisfied; very little evidence of dissatisfaction or complaint ever reaches the ears of top management. However, the danger of such an approach is that any suppressed feelings once it bottles up could suddenly flare up, proving disastrous to the organisation. Ultimately, they may decide to leave. Exit interviews may reveal the real reasons for their departure, though this is not always the case. Even where employees do 'tell all' at the exit interview, it is usually too late to do anything about their complaint or grievance and ask them to reverse their decision.

Beach also refers to several reasons why there should be a formal procedure to handle grievances:

- All employee complaints and grievances are in actual practice not settled satisfactorily by the first level supervisor, due to lack of necessary human relations skills or authority to act.
- It serves as a medium of upward communication, whereby the management becomes aware of employee frustrations, problems and expectations.
- It operates like a pressure release valve on a steam boiler, providing the employees with an outlet to send out their frustrations, discontents and gripes.
- It also reduces the likelihood of arbitrary action by supervision, since the supervisors know that the employees are able to protest such behaviour and make their protests heard by higher management.
- The very fact that employees have a right to be heard and actually heard helps to improve morale.

## The Benefits of a Grievance Handling Procedure

According to Jackson (2000), further benefits that will accrue to both the employer and employees are:

- It encourages employees to raise concerns without fear of reprisal.
- It provides a fair and speedy means of dealing with complaints.
- It prevents minor disagreements developing into more serious disputes.
- It saves employers time and money as solutions are found for workplace problems.
- It helps to build an organisational climate based on openness and trust.

Torrington & Hall refer to four key features of a grievance handling procedure.

Fairness: Fairness is needed not only to be just but also to keep the procedure viable, for if employees develop the belief that the procedure is only a sham, then its value will be lost, and other means sought to deal with the grievances.

Facilities for representation: There is also the risk that the presence of the representative produces a defensive management attitude, affected by a number of other issues on which the manager and shop steward may be at loggerheads.

Procedural steps: There is no value in having more just because there are more levels in the management hierarchy. This will only lengthen the time taken to deal with matters and will soon bring the procedure into disrepute.

Promptness: Promptness is needed to avoid the bitterness and frustration that can come from delay. When an employee 'goes into procedure,' it is like pulling the communication cord in the train.

Further, they should ensure that, if a grievance is not settled at the informal or first formal stage, workers have the right to have their grievances heard at further levels. All parties need to be satisfied that it is both fair in conception and application. It certainly should not be seen as a device for simply going through the motions. If a grievance is raised, then it is crucial that all parties have a desire to ensure that there is a fair hearing of the complaint and that, ultimately, justice is done.

## 7.2.1 The Steps in the Grievance Handling Procedure

The method by which formal grievances are processed varies with the labour contract. Glueck refers to 3 steps that apply to many, if not smaller enterprises. Initiation of formal grievance, Department head or unit manager and Arbitration.

1. Initiation of formal grievance: This step refers to the filing of the grievance. An aggrieved employee can file his grievance with the supervisor in the first instance, preferably in writing or at least initially orally, formulated if he wishes with the help and support of his union steward.

2. At this stage, the supervisor should make sure that the grievance is attended to and the problem solved, as soon as possible, without trying to assess the blame or find excuses. Joint attempt by him along with the union steward and the employee would be the most useful way of solving at this stage.

3. Department Head or Unit Manager: If the grievance cannot be solved at the level of the supervisor, it goes to the other level. The grievance must be presented in writing and both sides must document their cases. What this level consists of depends on the size of the organisation.

4. Arbitration: If the grievance cannot be solved at this intervening step or steps, an independent arbitrator may be called in to settle the issue. The arbitrator is generally experienced in labour management relations and often it is a labour lawyer, university professor of industrial relations or a former labour or management official now arbitrating full time. Arbitration provides a method for settling contractual disputes without having to resort to work stoppages.

Glueck states that most studies of grievances show that more than 75% are settled at the first step and another 20% at the next level. The rest, primarily in larger enterprises, are taken care of in the intervening steps. Relatively few studies have been done on grievances.

Dessler (2006) presents a set of guidelines to the managers in handling grievances. He says, 'As a manager, your behaviour in handling grievances is crucial. You are on the firing line and must, therefore, steer a course between treating employees fairly and maintaining management's rights and prerogatives.'

## Reducing Grievances and Improving the Process

It is impossible to remove grievances altogether from organisations. However, in view of the adverse effects grievances have on organisational effectiveness, measures should be taken to reduce them by adopting various approaches. Glueck refers to the following in this regard.

1. Reduce the causes of grievances such as bad working conditions or adopt a less employer-oriented supervisory style.
2. Educate managers on contract provisions and effective human relations oriented grievance processing.
3. Quickly and efficiently process all grievances
4. Encourage supervisors to consult personnel and other supervisors before processing grievances to get the best advice and improve effectiveness in the grievance process.

## 7.3. Introduction of Discipline

Discipline is the regulation of human activity to produce a controlled performance. The real purpose of discipline is quite simple: It is to encourage employees to meet established standards of job performance and to behave sensibly and safely at work. Discipline is essential to all organised group action.

Discipline is a procedure that corrects or punishes a subordinate because a rule or procedure has been violated. (Dessler, 2007)

Discipline should be viewed as a condition within an organisation whereby employees know what is expected of them in terms of the organisation's rules, standards and policies and what the consequences are of infractions. (Rue & Byars, 1996)

The purpose of discipline according to Dessler (2007) is to encourage employees to behave sensibly at work, where being sensible is defined as adhering to rules and regulations. In an organisation, rules and regulations serve about the same purpose that laws do in society; discipline is called for when one of these rules or regulations is violated

(Bittel & Newstrom, 1990). Following are some of the purposes and objectives of disciplinary action.

- To enforce rules and regulations

- To punish the offender
- To serve as an example to others to strictly follow rules
- To ensure the smooth running of the organisation.
- To increase working efficiency
- To maintain industrial peace
- To improve working relations and tolerance
- To develop a working culture which improves performance

Dessler (2007) say that a fair and just discipline process is based on three foundations: rules and regulations, a system of progressive penalties and an appeals process. These rules address things like theft, destruction of company property, drinking on the job and insubordination. The purpose of these rules is to inform employees ahead of time as to what is and is not acceptable behaviour. This is usually done during the employee's orientation.

## Grievance versus Discipline

When an employee is dissatisfied with management, he will initiate what is called a 'Grievance Handling Procedure' for redress. Similarly when the management is dissatisfied with an employee, 'disciplinary action' is initiated to correct the situation. Thus you see that discipline and grievances are two sides of the same coin. Whether a management or workforce member is dissatisfied, either situation requires the cooperation of union and management for its solution. The HR Department plays the leading role in both these cases because one profoundly influences motivation, morale, industrial peace and productivity in the organisation.

### 7.3.1 Approach to Discipline

Glueck (1978) states, 'the kind of discipline system used is normally related to the enterprise. It will be more formal in larger enterprises, especially those that are unionised. It is quite informal in smaller enterprises. How strict discipline is, depends in part on the nature of the prevailing labour market.

Human resources manager will try to diagnose in a disciplinary situation. For example, the supervisor may try to diagnose the difficult employee's motivation with a view towards improving performance. This is not always easy to do, and if the manager does not know the employee well because there are many employees or faces other conditions that work against her or him, it may be virtually impossible. Discipline is one of the most challenging areas in the personnel function, and the diagnostic approach rather than 'give her a fair trial before you hang her' approach is especially helpful in dealing with the difficult employee.

## Categories of Difficult Employees

Literature (Glueck, 1978; Ivancevich, 1998) refers to four categories of employees whose behaviour can be described as difficult.

Category 1: Those whose quality or quantity of work is unsatisfactory, as a result of to lack of abilities, training or job motivation.

Category 2: Those whose personal problems off the job begin to affect their productivity on the job. These problems can include alcoholism, drugs or family relationships.

Category 3: Those who violate laws while on the job by such behaviour as stealing from the organisation or its employees or physical abuse of employees or property.

Category 4: Those who consistently break company rules and do not respond to supervisory reactions.

## Discipline Approaches

Properly administered, discipline corrects as well as punishes and it helps to develop self control among employees. For most employees most of the time, the enterprise establishing and communicating clear rules and goals are enough to induce employees to be productive.

*Positive vs. Negative Approach*

Those in charge may rule with an iron hand, punish rule violators severely and in general force the members to obey and conform. This mode of leadership has been variously called negative discipline, punitive discipline, autocratic discipline or rule through fear. The other approach is to develop in people a willingness to obey and abide by the rules and regulations. They do so because they want to, not because they are afraid of the consequences of disobedience. This form of discipline is called positive or constructive discipline.

*The Preventive Approach:*

This emphasises prior analysis of employees, their work situations and probable relationships with supervisors to make sure that the match between job and employee is right. This is specifically done through strict screening at the recruitment and selection level.

*The Therapeutic Technique:*

When the preventive approach does not apply, counselling employees to let them know they are ineffective and to suggest how they might improve is in order. Many employees respond to this approach.

*The Self Improvement Programme:*

A variation of the therapeutic technique is for the supervisor to first document the employees' ineffectiveness and then encourage them to design a self-improvement program. This puts the emphasis where it belongs: on the employees, improving their performance with the supervisor's counsel and help.

*The Punitive Approach:*

When none of these methods works, corrective discipline is the last resort. These methods vary from warnings and oral reprimands to discharge or termination.

## 7.4. Disciplinary Process

The elements of a disciplinary process can easily be grasped from a simple illustration such as Figure 1. It is clear from the figure that the process starts by the employer initially establishing the rules and goals and then communicating them to employees. Employee behaviour is then assessed, and efforts are directed at modifying behaviour if found undesirable. This process is an attempt to prevent difficulties and is positive. It is designed to help employees succeed.

Figure I: Elements in a Disciplinary Process

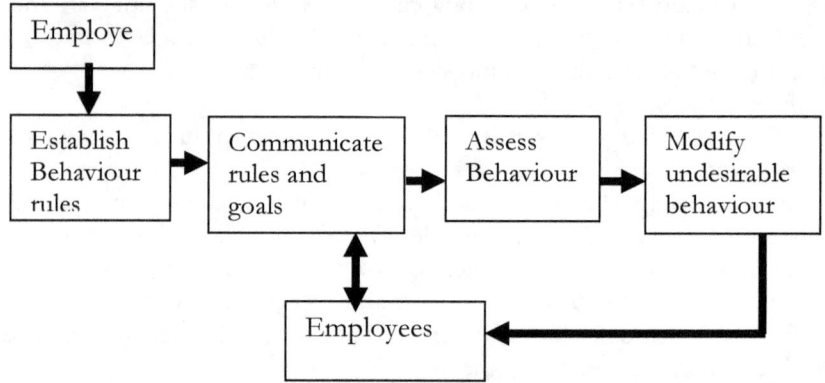

## Establishment of work and behaviour rules:

Through whatever method is used, a set of minimally acceptable work goals is established. Behaviour rules cover many facets of on-the-job behaviour. They can be categorised as concerning behaviour that is directly or indirectly related to work productivity. Rules directly related to productivity such as Time rules, Prohibited behaviour rules, Insubordination rules, Rules emphasizing laws and Safety rules. Rules indirectly related to productivity that are Prevention of moonlighting, Prohibition of gambling, Prohibition of selling or soliciting at work,

Clothing and uniform regulations, Rules about fraternization with other employees at work or off the job.

## Communication of the rules to all employees:

This is an important aspect of a disciplinary process. Employees must be convinced that the rules are fair and related to job effectiveness. Further, there needs to be a willingness to accept the rules and their enforceability. This can be promoted if the communication process is both clear and effective. Furthermore, if the employees or their representatives are also encouraged to participate in the formulation and revision of the rules, their cooperation with regard to both compliance and enforcement will most likely be assured.

## Assessment of Behaviour:

In most organisations, performance evaluation is the mechanism for assessing work behaviour deficiency. Rule-breaking behaviour usually comes to the attention of management when it is observed or when difficulties arise and investigation reveals certain behaviour as the cause.

## Modifying undesirable behaviour:

This element consists of a system of administering punishment or attempting to motivate change. This ranges from supervisory administration of discipline to formal systems like courts or grievance handling procedures.

### 7.4.1 Disciplinary Methods

As much as approaches are important, specific methodologies too are vital for the well being of the organisation. It should emphasises that discipline should be directed against the act rather than the person.

*Corrective and not punitive:*

The primary objective of disciplinary action is to correct the behaviour. Disciplinary proceedings and punishment must be seen as the 'means to an end' and not the 'end' itself. In other words, it must not be thought of as a punitive action. Only when corrective interventions prove ineffective should punitive measures be considered.

*Progressive actions and punishments:*

When punitive measures are required, first offences are dealt relatively minor punishments, to be followed by increasingly severe penalties should offences be repeated. A first offence, for instance, may receive simply an oral warning. Repeat offences will lead to increasingly harsh penalties and may even lead to a discharge or termination.

- Warning and oral reprimand
- First written reprimand
- Second written reprimand
- Suspension
- Discharge

*Natural justice:*

Principles of natural justice must be applied. Any disciplinary scheme must adhere to the concept of natural justice. This means that:

- Individuals must know the standards of performance they are expected to achieve and the rules to which they are expected to conform.
- They should be given a clear indication of where they are at fault or what rules they have broken.
- They should be given a chance to explain or explain themselves.
- No man should be a judge over his/her own case.
- Proceedings should not only be fair but also appear to be fair to all concerned.

*Hot Stove Rules':*

The application of discipline should be analogous to the burn received when touching a hot stove. The following are the 'hot stove rules' in disciplinary action. In other words, characteristics should be like the experience of being around a hot stove:

Immediacy: Immediate response upon infraction
Advance warning: Adequate warning
Consistency: Consistent response
Impersonality: Equality before the law

So how do managers put these guidelines into action? Glueck (p. 718) refers to a series of sanctions to improve future performance or behaviour. They vary from the brief fatherly or motherly chat to locking up the violator, as the military does on occasion. Suggestions and techniques suggested are

*Counselling:*

This is the most frequent method of disciplinary action. The supervisor determines if in fact a violation took place, explains to the employee why the violation significantly affects productivity and harmony in the workplace and suggests that it should not happen again. For most violations, this is all that is required. The counselling will probably be more effective if the supervisor applies the behaviour modelling –interaction management technique.

*Disciplinary Layoff:*

If the aforesaid measures do not help, the next step is normally a 'Disciplinary Layoff,' usually for a short period such as a few days up to a week. If damage results from the deviant behaviour, deductions may be made from the employee's pay over a period of time to pay for the damage, provided the laws in force allow such deductions.

*De-hiring:*

The next level of punishment is what is called 'De-hiring.' This is getting the employee to quit. It has many advantages over termination for both employer and employee. Both save face. The employee can find another job and then quit, telling the peer group how much better the new job is. The employer benefits from being rid of an ineffective employee without having to fire him or her.

*Discharge:*

The ultimate punishment is discharge. To some inexperienced managers, discharge is the solution to any problem with a difficult employee. But discharge requires that a case be made in support of it, both from the perspective of fairness and due process. Often, discharge is not possible, because of seniority rules, union rules, or too few replacements in the labour market or a number of other reasons. Discharge has many costs, both direct and indirect. Directly, a discharge leads to loss of all personnel investments already made in recruiting, selection, evaluation and training. Many organisations also provide severance pay. In addition to such direct costs, there are indirect costs, such as the effect on other employees.

## 7.4.2 Administration of Discipline

In unionised organisations, the employee has a formalised procedure that provides adequate protection. In non-unionised situations, the hierarchical system is the most prevalent. In other words, when an employer hires employees to work for an indefinite period of time and the employees do not have a contract limiting the circumstances under which they can be discharged, the employer can terminate the employees at any time for any reason or for no reason at all. These are employees at will. Have a closer look at these two situations.

## Formalized Disciplinary Procedures

In unionised enterprises, formalised disciplinary procedures are in place, as a result of bipartite agreements or tripartite agreements such as collective agreements. Disciplinary action is a quasi-judicial process. The procedure followed is greatly influenced by the socio legal systems prevailing in each country. They therefore differ from country to country, industry to industry, company to company.

In unionised organisations, collective agreements generally require the following in the administration of discipline:

- Preliminary investigation
- Framing of charges
- Issue of charge sheet and intimation
- Consideration of explanation
- Issue of show cause notice
- Notice of holding of inquiry
- Inquiry proceedings
- Award punishment
- Follow up

In many jurisdictions, many leading companies have adopted their own codes of discipline to ensure that they are committed to the principles of natural justice.

## Informal Disciplinary Procedures

*Hierarchical Disciplinary Systems:*

In non-unionised situations, informal discipline systems are the most prevalent. Discipline is administered to most non-unionised employees by the supervisor, who also evaluates the employee. When the employee is found to be ineffective, the supervisor decides what needs to be done. In this hierarchical system, the conditions allow a supervisor who might be arbitrary, wrong, or ineffective himself to be police, judge and jury over the employee. In such a situation, the penalty for an infraction of work rules may be the employee's job and salary. What can the employee do if his supervisor unfairly treats him? She or he could, of course, appeal to the supervisor's supervisor. But, this is often of no help at all as the whole value system of the hierarchy is based on supervisors supporting each other to build a good management team.

*Other Disciplinary Systems:*

Although the hierarchical discipline system is by far the most common in industry, employing organisations in other sectors used different models more often. The alternatives to the hierarchical model are described below.

*Peer Disciplinary Systems:*

The peer disciplinary system relies on independent or related peers to assess deviance and recommend behaviour modification. It has been used in some business organisations and professional organisations. Such systems can be implemented in several ways. A jury of peers to adjudicate is of course the method used in professional discipline situations such as disbarment of a lawyer or removal of a physician's license.

*Quasi-judicial Systems:*

Quasi-judicial systems involve independent outside persons to adjudicate cases. One example is the 'corporate ombudsman,' a person who is independent of the organisation and somewhat familiar with the law who can provide a fact finding mechanism and exercise independent judgment on the rights covered in disputes The role is similar to that of an arbitrator in unionised situations.

*Modified Hierarchical System:*

Regular appeal channels inside the organisation but including someone other than the supervisor's superior are used in the modified hierarchical discipline systems. One mechanism is to have all disputed dismissals or behaviour modification plans submitted to specified personnel specialists for conciliation and assessment Another is to have a top management executive or executives far removed from the scene hear the facts and judge whether proper action was taken. There are mechanisms that are a cross between a modified hierarchical system and a peer system.

*****

# 8 HEALTH AND SAFETY

## 8.1. Nature of Health and Safety

Up to last centuries, employers ran their businesses as they saw fit to make a profit. Employee safety and health were not their concern. In fact, in official terms these things were nobody's concern.

Significantly, the ILO in 1959 made recommendation No: 112, which provided that: 'Occupational health services should be established in or near a place of employment for the purpose of:

- Protecting the workers against any health hazard arising out of work or conditions in which it is carried on
- Contributing towards workers' physical and mental adjustment
- Contributing to establishment and maintenance of the highest possible degree of physical and mental well being of the workers'

Some businesses are large and profitable enough to employ specialists in Health & Safety. Smaller businesses employ consultants. The reason for this is that there are many hazards in any working place, with potentially far-reaching consequences, and expert knowledge is required to effectively identify and address them. If workers are injured or killed, the cost of workers' compensation insurance or similar coverage increases.

The costs of injuries and illnesses are innumerable to both employee and employer. Man-days are lost to an employer; there are losses in productivity and additional costs to be borne. The desire to reduce suffering, the need to contain direct and indirect costs of accidents, deaths and illnesses have moved organisations to create improved safe and healthy conditions at work.

Health Hazards are those aspects of work environment that slowly and cumulatively lead to deterioration of an employee's health; for example: cancer, poisoning and respiratory diseases. Typical causes include physical and biological hazards, toxic and carcinogenic dusts and chemicals and stressful working conditions.

Safety Hazards are those aspects of the work environment that have the potential of immediate and sometimes violent harm to an employee; for example, loss of hearing, eyesight, or body parts; cuts, sprains, bruises, broken bones; burns and electric shock.

## Factors Important to Health & Safety

Environmental, organisational and individual factors affect worker protection as: Nature of the Task, Employee Attitudes, Government, Trade Unions, Management's Goal, and Economic Conditions

Some jobs are more likely to cause injury than others: the very nature of the job is hazardous. Employee attitudes play a significant part in health and safety. If employees are committed to the idea of safety and cooperate with safety initiatives, then safety measures become more effective. Socially responsible managements had active Health & Safety programmes long before they were made mandatory by law. Some employers face the dilemma of ignorance about the consequences of some dangerous working conditions. Although work is being done to determine the dangers and to prevent or mitigate the consequences of such work, the costs of some of these preventive programmes are so high that it would not be economically viable to adopt them.

## Organisational Responses to Health and Safety

The larger organisations have set up safety departments usually under the purview of the human resources management team. Health and Safety must become the responsibility of everyone in an organisation if programmes are to be successful.

Safety committees in organisations prove very effective if everyone in the organisation gets involved in the work of the committee. This work covers the organisation's entire programme, i.e., inspection, design, record keeping, training and motivation.

## Safety Design and Preventive Approaches

Organisations have adopted measures to build-in safety through what is known as safety engineering. It makes jobs more comfortable, less confusing and less fatiguing. It keeps employees more alert and therefore less prone to accidents.

Safety engineers analyse all factors around jobs and as a result they are able to improve safety precautions. For example, protective guards for machinery and equipment, colour coding to indicate hazards or dangers, protective clothing/devises and belts/lifelines to prevent falls. They may also recommend suitable rest periods to increase safety as well as productivity, and also demarcate certain areas as being 'No smoking' or 'hard-hat' areas.

## Inspection, Reporting and Accident Research

Safety departments and specialists have another approach to reducing accidents and illnesses. They inspect the work place to find out:
- Are safety rules being observed?
- Are safety guards and protective equipment being used?
- Are there potential hazards in the work place that safety redesign could improve?
- Are there potential occupational health hazards?

Their observations and collected data then help them in setting things right. They would also investigate accidents or 'close calls', chiefly to ascertain what steps ought to be taken to prevent a recurrence. Reporting accidents and occupational illnesses is also an important part of the safety department's or specialist's job. Besides, OSHA requires that each 'recordable' incident be logged on an OSHA form. Under the act, a recordable incident is one, which resulted in:
- Death
- A non-fatal occupational illness
- An injury which caused loss of consciousness
- Restriction of motion or transfer to another job
- Required medical attention (other than first aid)

Safety and/or personnel specialists also carry out accident research at regular intervals during the work year. They systematically evaluate the evidence on accidents and health hazards. They gather data from both internal and external sources and also review available studies/findings that facilitate looking for hazardous conditions at the work place.

## Safety Training and Motivation Approaches

Safety training is usually part of the orientation/Induction programme for new employees. Training can also take place at any time during an employee's career. Although in safety as in other areas, workers often learn 'the ropes' from each other, some training is also required by government agencies. Those responsible for safety have also devised motivational devices such as safety contests and communication programmes in their efforts to create a safer environment for employees. They are intended to reinforce safety training.

## Auditing Safety Programmes

The National Safety Council in the US recommends a particular approach to accident prevention. It involves Engineering, Education and Enforcement. Stemming from this is a Safety Audit, A periodic inspection by safety specialists and/or committees to ascertain:

- to what extent safety prevails, and what lapses they observed
- any new hazard or potential threat to health

This in turn leads to an audit report that seeks to correct any threat to safety or health.

## Organisational Safety Programmes and Manager

The management of an organisation is primarily responsible for the safety of its employees. This does not mean that a worker is absolved from responsibility for his own safety and health. It only fixes the point of responsibility. Safeties being a team effort, managers have a responsibility to ensure that everyone cooperates to ensure that safety and health programmes are not only implemented but effective.

It must be noted that legislation and changed attitudes towards employees has made safety and health priority areas for managers. In their role of 'managing bottom lines' they should realize that support and commitment to safety and health is ultimately cost effective.

## Health Programmes for Employees

Larger organisations are likely to have their own medical and health facilities. The activities that are handled within these facilities vary from organisation to organization. but may include the following:

- treating accidents and medical emergencies at work
- performing physical examinations in conjunction with the selection of employees
- evaluating possible health hazards involved in transfers of employees to different regions or countries
- advising management on health hazards associated with the use of materials, chemicals in manufacture, or consumer usage of products
- Advising management on health-related problems of employees such as substance abuse and emotional problems
- Undertaking preventive medicine through periodic examinations and immunisation and group surveys for diabetes, cancer, TB and heart disease

Many of these functions are more important today than ever before due to far reaching government regulations. The extent of the facilities found in an organisation would depend on organisation size and the extent of health hazards on the job. Note however that health programmes are less widespread than safety programmes.

## 8.1.1 Occupational Diseases

### Causes of Occupational Accidents and Illnesses

- The task to be done – for example: poorly designed or repaired machines, lack of protective equipment, and presence of dangerous chemicals or gases.
- Working conditions – for example: excessive working hours that lead to fatigue, noise, lack of proper lighting, boredom, horseplay and fighting at work.
- The employee – for example, where the employee is accident-prone. Studies have shown that employees, who are under 30 years of age, lack psychomotor and perceptual skills, who are impulsive and easily bored, are more likely to have accidents than others.

Continuous exposure to a range of factors can seriously increase the probability of contracting occupational diseases. The list of harmful chemical, physical and biological hazards is a long one. It includes carbon monoxide, vinyl chloride, dusts, particulates, gases and vapours, radiation, excessive noise and extreme temperatures. When present in high concentration, these agents can lead to respiratory, kidney, liver, skin, neurological and other disorders.

### Typical Diseases

The potential sources of work-related diseases are distressingly varied as the way they affect the human organism. Schuler and Youngblood (1986) cites Ashford (1977) who says thus:

Typical health hazards include toxic and carcinogenic chemicals and dust, often in combination with noise, heat, and other forms of stress. Other health hazards include physical and biological agents. The interaction of health hazards and the human organism can occur either through the senses, by absorption through the skin, by intake into the digestive tract via the mouth or by inhalation into the lungs.

Schuler and Youngblood notes that OSHA is concerned with all of the following categories of occupational diseases and illnesses on which employers are required to keep records:

- Occupation-related skin diseases and orders
- Dust diseases of the lungs
- Respiratory conditions due to toxic agents
- Poisoning

- Disorders due to physical agents
- Disorders associated with repeated trauma
- All other occupational diseases

Following are some courses of action that organisations are already taking to protect their workforces from occupational diseases. Once the sources of harmful conditions on the job are identified, strategies to improve an organisation's occupational safety and health ratings can be developed. Some of the preventive and curative measures highlighted by the National Commission on Labour and other committees in India are the following

*Preventive measures:*
- Pre-employment medical examination
- Periodic post-employment medical examinations
- Removal of hazardous material/processes wherever possible
- Surveillance of employees exposed to health hazards
- Emergency treatment in case of accidents
- Availability of first-aid equipment
- Training employees in first-aid
- Education of employees in health and hygiene
- Special surveillance of the health of those more susceptible to disease
- Proper layout of factory and proper illumination
- Proper design of buildings with adequate ventilation
- Proper effluent disposal systems and/or treatment plants
- Careful design and selection of handling equipment
- Ergonomic design of work spaces and tools
- Proper design of job to remove monotony and fatigue
- Proper schedule of work with adequate rest periods
- Registration with BARC Trombay and their periodic inspection wherever radiation materials are used

*Curative measures:*
- Adequate medical treatment
- Allowing adequate time for convalescent rest and recuperation
- Adequate compensation.

## Occupational Accidents

Nair & Nair (1999) define accidents. Any occurrence taking place within the premises of industrial establishment arising out of and in the course of employment which is not planned or intended which might disrupt orderly progress of scheduled work and might cause injury or death to person(s) or result damage to equipment, material, buildings or infrastructure but exclude self inflicted personal injuries of employees of the organisation.

According to Dessler (2007) there are three basic causes of workplace accidents: chance occurrences, unsafe conditions and unsafe acts on the part of employees. Chance occurrences are more or less beyond management's control, so your responsibilities as a manager focus on unsafe conditions and unsafe acts.

## 8.1.2 Types of Accidents:

It is important that you understand the nature and types of accidents in the workplace. On the one hand it is necessary to prevent any injury to employees, and on the other, compensation to be paid to employees in the event of accident will depend on the type and nature of accident.

1.  Industrial injury – This is a personal injury to an employee which has been caused by an accident or an occupational disease and which arises out of or in the course of employment and which would entitle such employee to compensation under the laws of the land.
2.  Disablement – This is a loss of capacity to work or move due to an accident resulting in loss of reduction of earning capacity; it could be total, partial or temporary.
3.  Total disablement – This is a disablement whether of a temporary or permanent nature which incapacitates a worker for all work that he was capable of performing at the time of the accident.
4.  Partial disablement – This is a disablement that may be of a temporary or permanent nature, which reduces the earning capacity of a worker as a result of an accident.

## Causes of Accidents:

The causes of workplace accidents fall into four categories. The descriptions of these categories – intrinsic, extrinsic, personal and exogenous – should help you recognise how to prevent and manage the consequences of accidents:

Intrinsic Causes are those that reside in the jobs themselves. For example: Overexposure to radiation while working with X-ray and gamma ray machines.

Extrinsic Causes are relate to causes that are not of the job itself but arise from the environment in which the job takes place. For example: Lack of adequate lighting and ventilation that results in accidents

Personal Causes relate to accidents caused by the physical, mental, psychological and physiological state of the worker. They are causes that only the employee can control. For example: Lack of knowledge and skill and Psychological aspects such as forgetfulness, carelessness, indifference, lack of interest, day dreaming, frustration, anxiety, etc.

Exogenous Causes: Any causes not covered by the above are classified under this head and usually include 'Acts of God,' a phrase used to denote natural occurrences unconnected with human action or behaviour. Examples of these are lightening, floods and earthquakes.

According to Schuler and Youngblood accident prevention can also be seen as a function of how well people in an organisation communicate and work together. For example, the HR department must work with supervisors and managers in the recording of accidents. Effective records produced by both groups can highlight the causes of accidents as well as their severity and frequency.

## Cost of Accidents

The cost of accidents will vary with the type of accident, the nature of the injury or damage and location. Such costs will include direct and indirect costs.

*Direct costs include the following:*

- Cost of damages/destruction of equipment, machines, material and building and infrastructure involved
- Compensation paid to the injured worker or the estate of a dead worker
- Payment to injured worker during medical treatment and convalescence
- Cost of medical treatment of the injured
- Loss of production/wastage or inefficiency involved in case of replacement of injured worker with another less competent worker.

*Indirect costs include:*

- Loss of production until the injured person/equipment is replaced/substituted and production resumed
- Expenses incurred on persons such as Factory Inspectors/Engineers employed by government or company for improving safety standards and preventing accidents
- Loss of production time of other workers/supervisors/managers engaged in tasks associated with the accident, such as:
- sending the injured worker for medical attention
- investigating the cause of the accident and preparing reports
- attending proceedings of the investigation to the accident
- overheads during the period production is temporarily disrupted due to the accident.

## 8.2  Evaluation of Health and Safety

Major responsibility for occupational health and safety resides with the organisation and its management. Organisational safety and health programmes can have a much greater impact on employees' safety and health than government inspections can. Managers are there every day while the government inspector is not.

Odiorne (1971) suggests the following steps to develop a safety management programme:

- Establish meaningful systems of indicators
- Develop effective reporting systems
- Develop rules and procedures
- Reward supervisors for effective management of the safety function.

While management support for such a programme is necessary, none of it will prove effective unless the employees participate. Health and safety programmes can be evaluated directly through a cost-benefit type of analysis. The costs of safety specialists, new safety devices and other measures can be calculated. Reduction in accidents lowered insurance costs and lowered fines can be weighed against these costs.

Management can make a greater impact on health and safety at work than government or any outside agency can or ever will. For responsible, safety conscious managements, no cost/benefit ratio will ever have the same impact as that of safety efforts which prevented accidents, deaths and illnesses.

### Safety Organisation

At every level of management and supervision, there is a responsibility for the safety of those whom they supervise and the equipment under their purview. However, management alone cannot ensure safety without the cooperation of everyone in an organisation. Thus safety has to be everyone's responsibility. Management has to formulate comprehensive safety policies considering international standards, national policies and the interests of their business and employees.

### Safety Policy

The need for organisations to take a broader view of safety and health requires that they should formulate a clear policy on safety. In the UK, under the Health and Safety at Work Act of 1974,all organisations except those of less than five employees is required to prepare and keep up-to-date a written statements of their safety policies. These statements should reflect the employer's commitment to safety and health at work and indicate what standards of behaviour are to be aimed for in health, safety and welfare matters. The Act requires that the policy statement should be drawn to the attention of all employees. This means that focused attention must be given to ensure that employees have been given or made to understand the policy. For example, the policy could be dealt with at induction, or employees may be issued a booklet that contains the safety policy among other information about the organisation.

A holistic policy requires attention to at least the following
- the immediate workplace
- the adjacent community
- the regional environment
- the international environment.

A typical safety policy would include the following:
• A general statement about how the organisation looks at or deals with safety and health
• The safety organisation that would establish and maintain the structure of responsibility for safety and health matters throughout the company premises
• A statement on individual responsibility that would make every employee realise the need to be equally responsible for his own safety and that of those around him
• A review procedure by which the policy is reviewed periodically to ensure that it is relevant to current needs of safety and health in the organisation

It is the management's responsibility to develop a safety policy. In some countries this may be mandatory. More than a legal requirement, it educates the whole organisation on the need to pay attention to safety in the workplace. A policy helps the management and the employees to adhere to standard practices throughout the organisation.

## Work Stress

According to Ivancevich (1998) stress is a common experience that is part of everyone's life. It can be good for a person: called end stress, good stress is what helps a person complete a report on time or generate a good, quick, problem-solving procedure. Unfortunately, stress can also be a major negative aspect of the workplace. Heneman et al (2000) say that some employees may not feel capable of adequately responding to demands of their job and the work environment and when this happens employees are said to experience job stress. As a result, they may have a number of adverse reactions to it.

Stress can be defined as a person's physical, chemical and mental reactions to stressors or stimuli in the environment.(Ivancevich 1998) Other experts (Cooper and Payne, 1988) view stress in terms of physiological or body reactions: blood pressure, heart rate, or hormone levels.

Stress in individuals can be defined as any interference that disturbs a person's healthy mental and physical well-being. It occurs when the mind or body is required to perform beyond its normal capabilities. The results of stress may be harmful to individuals, families, society and organisations. Not surprisingly, the complexity and expectations typical of organisations can impose 'organisational stress.'

*Stress affects –*
- Society – and brings pressure on public services
- Individuals – and brings on illness and behavioural problems
- Industry – and causes industrial accidents and inefficiency.

Globalisation and technological advances have increased the speed at which employees are now required to work. Besides, liberalisation and the recent spate of worldwide acquisitions and mergers have brought in its wake large-scale retrenchment that in turn has spawned stress induced industrial illnesses. In other words, it has increased stress among those employees.

## Sources and Causes of Stress

some employees withstand stress much better than others and that for a given situation or factor, the stress levels varies widely between different individuals. Say for instance, a threat of retrenchment may make one person crestfallen and highly tensed; another person may take the same situation in her stride—a spur to looking for another job. the sources and causes of stress in three broad categories:
- Environmental factors
- Organisational factors
- Individual factors

Organisations can help by introducing meaningful efforts to mitigate or eliminate work stress from their organisations. Here are some of them:
- Carrying out stress audits: Data pertaining to the working climate, role stress, job satisfaction or frustration levels are gathered and analysed. An attitude or morale survey is one method. Mass interviews, counselling and exit interviews are sources of good information.

- Using scientific inputs: Information on causes, symptoms and consequences of work stress is collected and employees are educated to overcome the ill effects of work stress.
- Providing medical assistance: Progressive organisations obtain the services of doctors and psychologists to advise them on the causes of work stress in their organisations and recommend preventive measures. They also identify physiological, psychological and psychosomatic symptoms of work stress and help both individuals and organisations overcome their effects.
- Education and training: Publicity to create awareness on the causes of, effect on and remedies for work stress is given through educational and training inputs.

While it is essential that organisations take the mentioned measures to minimise work-related stress, the individual workers have an equal responsibility to deal with this issue.

The whole issue of stress can be well managed by managers throughout the organisation. It is not a sole responsibility of the HR manager or his department. However, the HR department has a role to play in programmes for coping with stress. It can provide specialists, facilities, monitoring or evaluation, and certain other important resources. World over, more and more organisations have become concerned about and have involved in stress management. In Japan, stress at work is alarming giving rise to a phenomenon called 'stress death'

## 8.3 Occupational Health and Safety in Sri Lanka

In most jurisdictions, laws make employers liable for practices that endanger the health and safety of workers. By establishing a mandatory minimum level of protection against occupational hazards, these laws help to standardize the basis on which businesses compete, as you see from the following information about the laws of occupational health and safety in Sri Lanka.

### Industrial Safety

As mentioned earlier, the principal enactment relating to occupational health and safety in Sri Lanka is the Factories Ordinance. There is no equivalent of the American OSHA in the country. However, the Factories Ordinance enacted in 1942 (as amended) provides for Health, Safety & Welfare.

Under the general provisions on health, the ordinance addresses matters such as:
- Cleanliness

- Overcrowding
- Ventilation
- Lighting
- Drainage of floors
- Sanitary conveniences
- Medical supervision.

Under the general provisions on safety, the Ordinance covers safe use of prime movers, transmission machinery, unfenced machinery hoists, lifts, cranes, etc. The list is lengthy but may need revision on the light of more advanced machinery being available now.

In terms of welfare, the Ordinance prescribes the provision of (safe) drinking water, washing facilities, resting facilities for female workers, first aid, fire escapes, removal of dust/fumes, etc.

The Ordinance further prescribes the maximum hours of work per day and week (48 hours a week excluding meals and rest and not more than 12 hours a day).

Non-compliance with the provisions makes the employer criminally liable.

While the Factories Ordinance applies to employees in factories, the Shop & Office Employees Act applies to employees in shops and offices (white collar employees) and provides for such matters as annual holidays, leave, lighting, ventilation, sanitary conveniences, washing facilities, intervals for rest or a meal.

Like the Factories Ordinance, the Act prescribes the maximum hours of work per day and week (8 hours a day and a maximum of 45 hours a week).

Supplementing these laws are enactments that deal with

- The employment of women, young persons and children
- The employment of females in mines
- Employees' holidays
- Maternity benefits.

## Workmen's Compensation

The Workmen's Compensation Ordinance (1934) provides for the payment of compensation by the employer to workers who sustain personal injury in certain circumstances.

Liability arises when the following conditions are satisfied:

- A worker earns a prescribed wage.
- A master-servant relationship exists between employer and worker at the time of the accident.

- The accident has arisen from and out of the course of employment. Provision is also made for compensation when an occupational disease is contracted.
- The absence resulting from the accident is over 7 days.

The term 'accident' has not been defined but it seems that it generally means some unexpected event or happening without design, even though there may be negligence. The Ordinance will not apply in respect of any injury (except death) caused by an accident directly attributable to 'fault' on the part of the worker. Fault in this regard is clearly defined.

The amount of compensation payable takes the form of a lump sum payment calculated in terms of the rules laid down in the Ordinance. The compensation payable is only for the results of the injury and not for the injury itself. The 'results of the injury' relevant to the calculation of the amount of compensation payable are clearly laid down and includes such topics as death, permanent and partial disablement, etc.

The amounts of compensation are in lieu of the wages and normally would be payable to the worker if he or she had attended work or had been given leave of absence with pay. The employer is under no obligation to pay wages in addition to the compensation.

## Health and Wellness Programmes

Worldwide, businesses are implementing corporate health/wellness programmes to improve the quality and productivity of their employees, by improving employees' health and wellbeing. The majority of work-site wellness programmes are employer financed with the money saved through reductions in employee ill health, as a result of the programme implementation in the longer-term. The potential benefits commonly attributed to work-site wellness programmes include an enhancement of corporate image, the selective recruitment of premium employees, a reduction of employee turnover, an increase of productivity, less absenteeism, a reduction in medical claims, and a reduced incidence of accidents and industrial injuries (Pelletier, 2001; Poole, Kumpfer, & Pett, 2001; Shephard, 1996). Such programmes have been found to be beneficial not only for the employee but also for the employer and the business as a whole.

The design, implementation and evaluation of corporate wellness programmes can be a very rewarding vocation for occupational therapists. Targeting the workplace makes sense, as one third of the populations waking hours are spent at work, where communication is organised and peers exert both support and pressure (Glasgow, Mccaul, & Fisher, 1993; Reardon, 1998). Work-site health promotion programmes are a primary means of preventing chronic diseases that are becoming more and more prevalent in today's society. Occupational therapists have the means to implement a holistic approach to corporate wellness programmes. Wellness is defined as 'a composite of physical, emotional, spiritual, intellectual, occupational, and social health.' Occupational therapists can implement programmes in the workplace that focus on all of these aspects of health.

Health and wellness programmes may include health risk assessment, smoking and alcohol reduction/cessation, blood pressure control and treatment, weight control, exercise and fitness, nutrition, back problem prevention and care, and stress management (Kasl & Serxner, 1992). Health and wellness programmes are trying to assist employees to be agents of change and educated consumers of health (Peters, 1994).

The choice to implement a workplace wellness program lies in the hands of the employer, as long as they are fulfilling their occupational health and safety obligations. Wellness is an issue that cuts across the entire organisation. One key to successful planning lies in surveying workers to identify health risks and the types of programmes that appeal to all employees (Litvan, 1995). It has been well established that resources committed to prevention have a multiplier effect on the resources expended on fixing the problem (Downey, Kudar, & Randolph, 1995).

*Perception and Participation*

It is evident that the employees need to know that their organisation is seriously concerned about their health. Ideally the employees need to be afforded the flexibility necessary to participate in the worksite health programme. Employees need to perceive that their senior management, supervisors and co-workers have positive attitudes towards health since these factors have all been associated with improved employee health status (Pelletier, 2001).

Wellness programmes promote health awareness. They impart knowledge of present and future consequences of behaviours and lifestyles and the risks they bring about. These programmes do not eliminate symptoms and disease; instead they attempt to bring about changes in lifestyles that enable employees to realise their full mental and physical potential. Note that wellness programmes focus on prevention while Employee Assistance Programmes focus on rehabilitation.

*Health promotion is a four- step process:*
*   Employees are educated on health risk factors.
*   Each employee's specific health risk factors are identified
*   Employees are helped to eliminated or reduce their risks through healthier lifestyles and habits

- Employees are helped to maintain their 'new' healthier life styles through self monitoring and evaluation.

The most popular programmes thus far have been smoking cessation, blood pressure control, cholesterol reduction, weight control/fitness, and stress management. Including families in these programmes is important to consider, as family problems such as lack of day care, marital disputes, financial difficulties, and adolescent alcohol and emotional disturbances also affect productivity at work, causing absenteeism, tardiness, inattentiveness, and poor work quality (Pelletier, 2001).

All this leads to the question whether programmed wellness efforts can indeed reduce health care costs. Certainly, health promotion programmes have been seen to eliminate or reduce health risk factors, and these changes have been long-lasting. There is mounting evidence, for example, of a reduction in heart disease through increased awareness of the ill effects of smoking and the consequent change in habits. However, insufficient evidence has accumulated to show that the costs are justified. Insert chapter eight text here. Insert chapter eight text here. Insert chapter eight text here. Insert chapter eight text here. Insert chapter eight text here.

*****

# 9 INDUSTRIAL AND LABOUR RELATION

## 9.1 Industrial and labour relation

The 'work dominates the lives of most men and women' and 'the management of employees, both individually and collectively, remains a central feature of organisational life.' Blyton and Turnbull (1994) Industrial or labour relations the terms are often used interchangeably can be viewed as the interaction between the various interested parties involved in employment. The employer and employee are obvious parties. The state, in ensuring a level playing field for both sides, provides the legal framework within which such relations may take place.

A notable body of thought about labour relations was that of J. T. Dunlop, who applied the systems concept to industrial relations in 1958. Dunlop's systems approach model sees industrial relations as a subsystem of society distinct from, but overlapping, the economic and political subsystems. The model has four interrelated elements:

- Actors – management, non-managerial employees and their representatives and specialised government agencies concerned with industrial relations.
- Contexts – influences and constraints on the decisions and actions of the actors which emanate from other parts of society
- Ideology – beliefs within the system, which not only define the role of each actor or but also, define the view that they have of the role of the other actors of the system.
- Rules – the regulatory framework, developed by a range of processes and presented in a variety of forms, which expresses the terms and nature of the employment relationship.

Labour relations is a continuous relationship between a defined group of employees (represented by a union or association) and an employer. The relationship includes the negotiation of a written contract concerning wages, hours and other conditions of employment and the interpretation and administration of this contract over its period of coverage. (Milkovich & Glueck, 1985)

Industrial relations is a set of phenomena, operating both within and outside the workplace, concerned with determining and regulating the employment relationship. (Salamon, 1998). The nature of industrial relations has evolved from early origins in the master-servant relationships of the trades when overall power resided with the owner/employer. Many factors in the changing nature of organisations and society, especially in the last 100 years, have produced the forms of relationships seen today.

The period since the mid 1980s has seen significant developments in management's approach to industrial relations. No single strategy has been adopted by organisations, but certain strands are apparent:

- Management initiative: Management has been the prime mover for introduction of HRM approaches and projects intended to support and be integrated with the achievement of business objectives.
- Process relationships: The balance has shifted from an emphasis on the management/union relationship (collectivism) to an emphasis on the management/employee(s) relationship (individualism).
- Structure of bargaining: There has been a continuation of the shift from the national 'multi-employer' level to the 'single-employer' organisational level.
- Pay and working arrangements: The new emphasis among most organisations has been on 'flexibility' and greater individualisation of the contractual relationship.

The post Industrial Revolution era and the post Depression period saw a steep rise in the strength of unions. The ability of the unions to bring society to focus on the poor living standards of workers and the large-scale unemployment of youth contributed in no small measure to the growth of trade unions worldwide.

## Objectives of Industrial Relations (IR)

Nair & Nair also cite Kirkaldy (1947), according to whom there are four objectives for IR:

- improvement of economic conditions of workers
- State control on industries for regulating production and promoting harmonious industrial relations.
- socialisation or rationalisation of industries by making State itself a major employer.

• vesting of the proprietary interest of the workers in the industries in which they are employed.

Given these overall goals and objectives, it is not surprising that the field is engaged in a number of policy- and operations-oriented activities. Still another area to which industrial relations activities contribute significantly is that of overall industrial goals such as productivity, labour peace, and industrial democracy.

*Employer to Individual Employee Relationships:*
This relates to the areas of management focus in relation to policies and practices that ultimately affect the productivity and well being of their employees as individuals. With a view to optimising the interests of the employer and those of employees, these comprise fields such as: Wages & Salary administration, Career prospects inclusive of planning and promotion, Retirement benefits and medical benefits, Discipline & redress of grievances, Training & Development, ect.

*Labour Management Relations:*
Distinct from Employer-Employee relations is this area, which relates to relations between the employer as a management body and its workers as a recognised group or set of groups. It covers rights, protocols and practices, often regulated by a legal structure, related to management, formation and recognition of unions to represent the interests of the employees, collective agreements and the settling of industrial disputes.
Through these bodies, management and labour negotiate and enforce the establishment of welfare measures and benefit schemes. Another focus of labour-management relations are health and safety regulations and programmes at work.

*Industrial Peace & Productivity:*
One of the most important aspects of IR is to maintain industrial peace and thereby increase productivity. It depends on the quality of the union-management relations at workplaces. In fact, proactive labour administrations of some countries have changed their focus from being a law enforcer to a facilitator to maintain industrial peace. Productivity is another important area in which IR becomes significant. In the highly competitive area of global business maintaining high productivity is important for the survival of organisations. In the Global Competitiveness Report 2001-2002, this fact is borne out well. A few other areas of focus for Industrial Relations are:
-    Upgrading technology and production methods

- Securing employee commitment and cooperation in improving productivity
- Minimising 'man days lost' per year
- The retraining and redevelopment of surplus labour

*Industrial Democracy:*

The nature of the relationship between employees and management in the organisation's decision making process is central to the character and conduct of the industrial relations system at the organisational level. Industrial democracy is also known as worker's control (Salamon, 1998). this is a socio-political concept or philosophy of industrial organisation, which focuses on the introduction of democratic procedures to restructure the industrial power and authority relationship within organisations. The central objective of industrial democracy is the establishment of employee self-management within an organization.

## 9.1.1 The International Labour Organisation (ILO)

The ILO is the international institutional framework which made it possible to address issues such as the eight-hour working day, maternity protection, child labour laws and a range of policies that promoted workplace safety and peaceful industrial relations – and to find solutions allowing working conditions to improve everywhere. No country or industry could have afforded to introduce any of these in the absence of similar and simultaneous action by its competitors.

*The ILO has four main objectives:*
1. To promote and realise standards and fundamental principles and rights at work
2. To create greater opportunities for women and men to secure decent employment.
3. To enhance the coverage and effectiveness of social protection for all
4. To strengthen tripartism and social dialogue.

In 1944, the International Labour Conference met in Philadelphia USA, and adopted the Declaration of Philadelphia which redefined the aims and purposes of the ILO through the adoption of the following principles:
- Labour is not a commodity
- Freedom of expression and of association are essential to sustained progress
- Poverty anywhere constitutes a danger to prosperity everywhere

- All human beings, irrespective of race, creed or sex have the right to pursue both their material well being and their spiritual development in conditions of freedom and dignity, of economic security and of equal opportunity

In 1988, the ILO Conference adopted the 'Declaration on Fundamental Principles and Rights at Work', which re-affirmed the commitment of the international community to 'respect, to promote and to realise in good faith' the rights of workers and employers to freedom of association and the effective right to collective bargaining.

## 9.2 Labour Legislation

During the last two decades, a large number of labour laws has been enacted, particularly in the developing world. India tops the list in amount of labour legislation. In the UK, the 1970s saw increased legal intervention into industrial relations. In the US, until about 1930 there were no special labour laws (Dessler, 2001).

Employers were not required to engage in collective bargaining with employees and were virtually unrestrained in their behaviour toward unions. This one-sided situation lasted from the Revolution to the Great Depression. Since then, in response to changing public attitudes, values, and economic conditions, labour law has gone through three clear changes: from 'strong encouragement' of unions, to 'modified encouragement coupled with regulation,' and finally to 'detailed regulation of internal union affairs.' (Dessler, 2001)

When you look around the world, particularly the developing countries, you would notice that labour legislation has been quite influenced by the politics of the day. If the political party in power is pro-labour, then you will see the government's labour administration becoming more and more protective of the country's labour force. This is done through the introduction of pro-labour laws into the statute book.

## 9.2.1 Types of Legislation

Much of the legislation is sector based, such as factories, and is related to physical and other working conditions, such as hours of work, minimum lighting and space, overtime, maximum hours of work, etc., particularly pertaining to work in factories. Many countries would have a 'Factories Act' that deals with all these aspects. Similarly, there are laws that specifically deal with employment of persons in Shops and Offices and other sectors of industry. These types of legislation also may deal with areas such as maternity benefits and the prevention of child labour.

There are minimum wages and terms and generic conditions of employment prescribed in some countries, such as some in the Asian region, where social security measures are non-existent. Laws may also provide for the period of time within which salaries/wages have to be paid.

Laws may prescribe the whole gamut of industrial relations that includes dispute settlement, industrial courts/tribunals and their powers, and the ability of the state to refer such disputes for settlement to specified bodies. A country's laws usually provide for rules and regulations pertaining to trade unions. They would deal with such areas as the formation and registration of trade unions and the recognition of such unions by employers, as well the as the rights, powers, and duties of the unions, etc.

## Industrial Disputes/Conflicts

In the applicable Indian law, industrial disputes are defined rather circularly as: 'Any dispute or difference between employers and employers or between employers and employees or between employers and employees which is connected with the employment or non-employment or the terms and conditions of employment or with the conditions of work of any person' (Indian Industrial Disputes Act of 1947).

The definition includes three different possible sets of antagonists in industrial conflict. However, the present discussion is confined to disputes arising between management and workers. Disputes arise from a variety of sources for a variety of reasons. Some are innocent misunderstandings of regulations or policies but others are much more complicated, sometimes with malicious intent. In some cases, the cause lies with the individual manager or employee but others are due to management union intent. The following sections review the various causes under two categories: conflicts caused by unions and those caused by management.

## Conflict Caused by Unions:

The quality of the relationship also depends on the people who interact for the two parties, meaning those in the management and the trade union officials. In some countries the trade unions are also politicized and as a result even if the relationship between the management and the unions are free of conflict, political interference may disturb the relationship and give rise to conflict situations. Some of the situations that may arise as a result are: Non-cooperation, Absenteeism, alcoholism or a high incidence of accidents, Strikes etc.

## Conflict Caused by Management:

In a unionised setting, managers can create their share of conflict. Many are the court cases that were the result of a heated argument between 'Personnel' and workers over trivial issues. Some of the causes are outlined below. Refusal to discuss or negotiate a demand by the union is a very common cause resulting in a dispute. Also, a manager may use derogatory language on an employee resulting in sections of employees walking out in protest until that manager tender a public apology. Some causes may emanate from disciplinary issues that result in suspension, demotion, dismissal etc. A few other causes are layoffs, lock out, and termination.

## Causes of Disputes

Many factors can precipitate disputes. Nair & Nair (1999) have classified them:

- Economic causes – wages salaries, profit etc.
- Social causes – low morale, corruption, pollution, rising unemployment etc
- Political causes – political rivalry, unstable government etc
- Technical causes – fear of losing jobs due to automation, unsuitable technology etc
- Psychological causes – loss of job, propaganda, instigation etc
- Market causes – competition, loss, recession etc
- Legal causes – court order of closing down factories, shifting (under zoning laws)

Most of these causes would be seen to be at macro level beyond the realm of management or labour control. However, where managements and workers do have control is at the micro level where the quality of their relationships, mutual trust and respect enhance the sense of belonging, commitment and interest in the job. Good industrial relations will thus be seen as the key to greater productivity on the one hand leading to greater profits for the employer while giving employees a better quality of life through better earnings.

## Resolution of Conflict/Disputes

The need to contain industrial strife has led to many means for resolving disputes, all of which fall into one of three classifications which are elaborated below:
- Labour Administration by the state
- Statutory measures

• Non-statutory measures

*Labour Administration:*

The Labour Ministry or Department in some of the Asian countries lays down policy guidelines on labour matters. The government passes laws enabling government machinery to intervene in labour disputes. In some countries, provincial governments also have the power to enact legislation in respect of labour matters in their countries.

The Asian labour administrative context is different in view of a different social and legal regime. The state machinery ensures the implementation of the country's laws and intervenes to settle disputes.

*Statutory Measures:*

Most countries also set up statutory bodies to deal with the settlement of disputes. These are somewhat different from government labour administration agencies such as departments or ministries of labour or manpower. These have authority, conferred by labour laws, to settle disputes. In some disputes the labour department or ministry may appear before court as a facilitator.

In India and Sri Lanka the principal enactment is the Industrial Disputes Act of each country. In Sri Lanka however, numerous other laws have added to statutory measures in the settlement of disputes. Some of them are: Industrial Courts, Labour Tribunals and Arbitration.

*Non-statutory Measures:*

Most disputes can be resolved short of going before a legally constituted body such as the labour tribunal or industrial courts. Voluntary arbitration, workers' participation in management and collective bargaining are some of the key measures in this regard. One of the chief measures in this area in India is the Code of Discipline formulated by the Indian Labour Conference in New Delhi in 1957 for Indian Industries. Worker participation in management and collective bargaining are the other measures available in India and Sri lanka.

## 9.3 Introduction of Trade Unionism

Trade Unionism has its roots in Marxist dogma. It began as a force to counter the exploitation of workers by the newly established post Industrial Revolution 'capitalists' whose actions widened the gap between the living standards of owners and workers. Trade unionism can be mutually beneficial if a responsible partnership exists, but can be destructive and counterproductive if both sides consider themselves adversaries to each other. Here is the definition of a trade union from the Indian Trade Unions Act of 1926:

'Any combination of persons, whether temporary or permanent, primarily for the purpose of regulating the relations between workers and employers or between workers and workers or for imposing restrictive conditions on the conduct of any trade or business and includes the federations of two or more trade unions.'

A non-legislative definition of a union is:

'An organisation of workers acting collectively who seek to protect and promote their mutual interests through collective bargaining.' De Cenzo & Robbins (1993)

In Sri Lanka, our Trade Union Ordinance (1935) defines a Trade Union as follows:

"Trade Union means any association or combination of worker or employers, whether temporary or permanent, having among objectives one or more of the following objectives;

- The regulation of relations between workmen and employers, or between workmen and workmen or between employer and employers;
- The imposing of restrictive conditions on the conduct of any trade or business;
- The representation of either workmen or employers in trade disputes;
- The promotion or organization of financing of strikes or lockouts in any trade or industry or the provisions of pay or other benefits for its members during a strike or lockout, and includes any federation of two or more unions"

So why do workers form unions? What are the underlying principles of trade unionism? Today, to a large extent, three maxims provide the underlying principles of trade unionism.

*'Unity is strength'*

The early capitalists were able to exploit workers, as the worker was on an unequal footing vis-à-vis his employer, i.e., he had no bargaining power. When workers realised that their strength lay in numbers they were able to win for themselves concessions that would not have been possible but for their collective might. This was probably the first principle of trade unionism.

*'Equal pay for equal work'*

Unions believe that caste, creed, sex or race should never form the basis of discrimination against a worker. If equal work is done, then the pay should also be equal. This also provides for the elimination of any discrimination of workers. In the past when paternalism was practiced, the owner-employer had his favourites and they were treated better than others who did the same kind of work. This is not possible now as trade unions are very vigilant about job contents of its members and those who haven't joined the union.

'*Security of employment*'

One of the major principles of Trade Unionism is to safeguard the security of employment of the members. When employers try to retrench, lay off or downsize, unions vehemently protest to save the jobs of some of their members. Such action from a union is somewhat protective of its own membership lists. There have been instances where members have left one union and joined another which could put up a better fight for their welfare.

## 9.3.1 Classification of Trade Unions

So far, the concept of unions has been discussed as almost a single topic. In actual fact, there are variations on the theme: unions are of various types and serve various purposes, as the following three sections describe.

### Classification Based on Trade

Many unions have memberships and jurisdictions based on the trades they represent. The most narrow in membership is the craft union, which represents only members certified in a given craft or trade, such as pipe fitting, carpentry, and clerical work. Although very common in the western world, craft unions are not common in countries like India & Sri Lanka.

At the other extreme in terms of the range of workers represented is the general union, which has members drawn from all trades. Most unions in India & Sri Lanka are in this category.

Another common delineation of unions based on trades or crafts is that between so-called blue-collar workers and white-collar workers. Unions representing workers employed on the production floor, or outdoor trades such as in construction work, are called blue-collar unions. In contrast, those employees in shops and offices and who are not in management grades and perform clerical and allied functions are called white-collar workers

In addition, trade unions may be categorised on the basis of the industry in which they are employed. Examples of these are workers engaged in agriculture or forestry: hence agricultural labour unions or forest worker unions.

*Classification Based on Agreement*

Another basis on which labour agreements are sometimes distinguished is on basis of the type of agreement involved, based on the degree to which membership in the union is a condition of employment

Closed Shop: - Where management and union agree that the union would have sole responsibility and authority for the recruitment of workers, it is called a Closed Shop agreement. The worker joins the union to become an employee of the shop. The Taft-Hartley Act of 1947 bans closed shop agreements in the USA, although they still exist in the construction and printing trades. Sometimes, the closed shop is also called the 'Hiring Hall.'

Union Shop: - Where there is an agreement that all new recruits must join the union within a fixed period after employment it is called a union shop. In the USA where some states are declared to be 'right-to-work' states, the union shop is prohibited – i.e., anyone, irrespective of union membership, has the 'right to work'.

Preferential Shop: - When a Union member is given preference in filling a vacancy, such an agreement is called Preferential Shop.

Maintenance Shop: - In this type of arrangement no compulsory membership in the union before or after recruitment exists. However, if the employee chooses to become a member after recruitment, his membership remains compulsory right throughout his tenure of employment with that particular employer. This is called a maintenance of membership shop or maintenance shop.

Agency Shop: - In terms of the agreement between management and the union a non-union member has to pay the union a sum equivalent to a member's subscription in order to continue employment with the employer. This is called an agency shop.

Open Shop: - Membership in a union is in no way compulsory or obligatory either before or after recruitment. In such organisations, sometimes there is no union at all. This is least desirable form for unions. This is referred to as an open shop.

The above classifications are more usual in the west than on the Indian sub-continent.

*Classification Based on Membership*

This type of classification exists mostly in India especially in the states of Maharashtra & Gujarat. It is based on the Bombay Industrial Relations Act and derives from the membership on the roll of the union.

A 'Qualified Union' is one with less than 5% of the total employees, while a 'Representative Union' is one that has at least 15% of the total employees and a 'Primary Union' is one which has more than 15% of the employees on its roll.

## Evolution of Trade Unions

The Industrial Revolution in the 19th century brought about massive increases in output. It gave the owners of businesses an equally massive increase in capital accumulation. It did very little to improve the lot of the average worker. Wages were low, working conditions abominable and hazardous. Labour was considered a commodity that could be bought or sold.

The first visible union activity in the USA took place in 1794 when the shoemakers of Philadelphia made an attempt to increase their wages, which had been unilaterally reduced by their employers. The shoemakers were not successful and, in 1806, a federal court fined the union and ruled in favour of the employers, who contended that the combination of workers was an illegal conspiracy in restraint of trade. However, in a landmark case in 1842, (Commonwealth of Massachusetts v Hunt) the conspiracy theory was overturned and the court ruled that unions were not criminal per se as they could have honourable as well as destructive objectives. The unions' objective would determine whether it was legal or illegal.

After the Hunt decision, many unions emerged. In 1886 the American Federation of Labour (AFL) was organised. It was an amalgamation of national craft unions. It emphasised craft (rather than industry) and did not take on any particular political philosophy. Its objectives were more pragmatic than social or political.

In 1935, the Congress of Industrial Organisations (CIO) was formed. Although it was intended to work within the AFL, many issues forced the two apart. The CIO addressed all workers, not just those in crafts. However, the AFL and CIO merged later, in 1955, and became a formidable force in collective bargaining country-wide in the States.

In Sri Lanka, the first Trade Union of Sri Lanka formed as "Ceylon Printers Society" in 1893. The Ceylon Printers Society is also the first trade union to be formed in the whole of South East Asia.

Trade Union Ordinance (No. 14 of 1935) was promulgated in 1935. The first trade union to be registered under the Trade Union Ordinance was, however, not an association or workers but the Employers Federation of Ceylon. The workers associations were suspicious of the intentions of the government in requesting registration of trade unions. Hence, they were reluctant to register with the Ordinance initially. The first workers association to be registered was the Sri Lanka Chanffeurs Association, which was registered in 31st January 1936. Later many other trade unions came forward to register. By 1936, 28 unions had been registered and today closer to 1800 trade unions are in force. In 1948 the Trade Union Ordinance was amended to allow public servants to form Unions.

## 9.3.2 The Trade Union as an Organisation

Unions are organisations and employers too. Like any other organisations, unions too have objectives. Their objectives may either be job-conscious or class-conscious.

Job Consciousness leads to relatively limited economic goals pursued through such mechanisms as collective bargaining. The labour movement in the USA pursues this objective. Class Consciousness, by contrast, seeks fundamental change in the political and economic system; unions obtain such change through the political arena. Even though in the US unions may endorse candidates and encourage their members to actively participate in the political process, their objectives still remain the economic betterment of their members. They do not seek an alternative economic or political system. However, such fundamental change may be the objective of the union movement in European or South American countries.

At the same time it is important to remember that even some trade unions are unaware of the contribution they can make to their organizations. In most instances, trade unions are more concerned about employee rights and demands and thus forget about the contribution they can make to the organization.

Advantages of having trade unions in organizations.
* Trade unions will make it easier for management to deal with employees.
* With the partnership of trade unions organizations can develop and implement better HR practices
* Trade unions ill bring employee problems to the notice of the management.
* Trade unions would provide a channel for communication for organizations. It is easier for organizations to communicate to employees through trade unions in some instances than individually.
* Trade unions will generate supportive suggestions for improving performance and efficiency of organizations

- If collective agreements are entered into, it would be easier to maintain discipline in the organization.

In order to gain these advantages both trade unions and management should act in good faith and without hidden agendas.

Yet, many of the Sri Lankan trade unions are politicalised and thus give priority to the accomplishment of their various political objectives. Not only do they overlook the contribution they can make to the organization, they also overlook various employee problems for which they should make a stand. This political interference in trade unions has led to lot of confrontations, violence and destructions, creating a very negative image about trade unions.

## Why Employees Join Unions

From a practical standpoint, people would join unions if the benefit they derive from being a member is greater than the cost of being a member. Therefore, potential increases in wages must be greater than the amount of dues paid. Thomas Kochan et al (1984) developed a model according to which an individual's decision to join or avoid a union is influenced by three critical determinants. They are:

- Perceptions of work environment
- Job dissatisfaction
- Working conditions problems
- Inequity perceptions
- Perceptions of influence
- Desired influence
- Difficulty of influencing conditions
- Beliefs about unions
- Big-labour image
- expectations about unions

There also has been research into the reasons employees give for not joining unions:

- They identify with management
- They do not agree with the goals of unions
- They see themselves as professionals and unions as inappropriate for professionals.

For a better relationship it is important for the management to identify the real reasons for formation of trade unions. In this endeavour recognizing why employees join trade unions and why employees reject

trade unions are significant. Employees may join trade unions for various reasons. Some of them are;
- Trade unions are a collective effort.
- Social factors.
- Political affiliations.
- To exercise leadership.
- Exploitation by the employer.
- Peer pressure.
- Absence of god employee employer relationship.
- To minimize favouritism and discrimination.

Why employees reject trade unions are;
- Social factors.
- Identification with the management.
- Fear of reprisal / punishment.
- The job satisfaction is another factor to reject trade unions
- Good terms and conditions of employment

## Problems of Trade Unions

Nair & Nair (1999) showcase the Indian situation quite vividly in presenting the problems of Indian trade unions. Some of these may also be relevant to other countries and particularly to the West. Let us look at each of these briefly.

Multiple trade unions: India has a problem in its trade union movement because of the very large number of unions. It has caused inter-union rivalry and compromised on the unity of workers. It also leads to fragmentation of the worker population. Some unions may be more than willing to accede to the pressures of the employers and some others may be in the hands of the politicians who are behind trade unions purely to expand their voter base than to look after the welfare of the workers.

Politicisation: In a democracy, political influence on trade unionism cannot be avoided. (Nair & Nair). In countries such as India and Sri Lanka, the historical development of the trade union movement was inseparably attached to the political movement through the struggle for independence. Although in the beginning it helped the unions to gain considerable influence on the government in power, in the long run it has become a threat to the unity of the working class.

Democracy and Leadership: Nair & Nair point out, with particular reference to India, that the basic objective of trade unions may be to promote industrial democracy but that in practice, it rarely happens. Union leaders show authoritarian behaviour with less than optimal participation, openness and transparency.

Lack of adequate finance: Large number of small sized unions find it extremely difficult to sustain themselves, as their only means of income is membership subscriptions. Poor finances affect union activities and when members are not adequately served, they tend to gravitate toward other unions. Those are the major reasons for failure of trade unions particularly in the Asian continent.

## 9.4 Collective Bargaining

You saw previously that workers united in order to win concessions from owner employers in the Post Industrial Revolution era. This unity offered them strength, and probably as a result, they found it very convenient to present their problems to management through their union. Managers also found it easier to deal with union leaders to resolve problems common to workers. This led to the concept of collective bargaining first identified by Sidney and Beatrice Webb in the UK and by Groper in the US. Collective bargaining grew with the growth of unionism.

Collective bargaining may be defined as: A method of determining terms and conditions of employment and regulating the employment relationship which utilises the process of negotiation between representatives of management and employees intended to result in an agreement which may be applied across a group of employees. Salamon (1998, 305)

The National Labour Relations Act of the USA reads:
For the purpose of (this act) to bargain collectively is the performance of the mutual obligation of the employer and the representative of the employees to meet at reasonable times and confer in good faith with respect to wages, hours, and terms and conditions of employment, or the negotiation of an agreement, or any question arising there under, and the execution of a written contract incorporating any agreement reached if requested by either party, but such obligation does not compel either party to agree to a proposal or require the making of a concession. (Dessler (2007)

As Dessler argues, this means in plain language that both management and labour are required by law to negotiate wages, hours, and terms and conditions of employment 'in good faith.' Bargaining in good faith is the cornerstone of effective labour management relations. It means that both parties communicate and negotiate. Collective Bargaining would thus be seen as a process whereby representatives of employers and employees negotiate, administer and enforce agreements that cover wages, hours of work and other terms and conditions of employment.

There is more to collective bargaining than the mere getting together of two bodies to review and agree upon certain terms of employment. Formally, collective bargaining involves the following:

- Statutory support by legislative measures
- The existence of employee representatives, i.e., the union
- The recognition of the union by the employer as the bargaining agent
- The existence of an industrial dispute
- The threat of economic force in the form of a 'lock out' or 'strike' to settle an industrial dispute or to reach an agreement
- Negotiation
- Finalisation of an agreement
- Implementation of an agreement

Collective bargaining can be a stabilising factor in the free enterprise system. The recognised representation of employees by the union and the prescribed practices of collective bargaining and is agreements provide an accepted means to solve economic conflict, a clear legal framework within which the parties negotiate and establishes an safety valve for psychological and social conflict among the individuals and groups involved.

To achieve a successful management-union relationship and the acceptance of collective bargaining protocols, a state of genuine representation and acceptance of the parties must exist. For such a relationship, what might be called the critical success factors (CSFs) are:

- The bona fide interaction of the two parties
- The union's understanding that the interests of workers are not superior to that of the survival and success of the organisation
- Managements must accept and support the rights of trade unions
- The union at the collective bargaining process must truly represent a majority of workers
- The union representatives must be purposeful but reasonable
- Managements must be progressive and enlightened. They must not exploit disunity among unions to their advantage
- Both managements and unions must be vigilant enough to prevent political exploitation of conflict for political ends

With these conditions in place, it is the hope of all concerned that timely and peaceful agreements can be negotiated and that disputes that arise are amicably settled. However, there are times and circumstances in which this is not the outcome, thereby leading to escalated conflict and the taking of more extreme measures available to the bargaining parties.

Collective bargaining in Sri Lanka is mainly limited to individual union's negotiating with individual organisations although a few collective agreements cover a number of employers and employees across many organisations and many categories of employees. For example: the Collective Agreement between the Employers' Federation of Ceylon and the Ceylon Mercantile Union commonly called the EFC/CMU Collective Agreement.

### 9.4.1 The Nature and Scope of Collective Agreements

A better understanding of the process will come from reviewing some of its critical ingredients:

- It is a group process
- It involves negotiation
- It is a bipartite exercise involving representatives of unions or associations of employees and employers
- The objective of collective bargaining is to reach an agreement
- The purpose of the process is to improve working conditions for employees while securing the interests of management
- It is not merely an economic process, it is a socio-economic process that involves mutual respect of each other's views, aspirations, expectations, and values
- It meticulously follows legislation, rules, regulations, conventions and customs developed by trade unions, managements, corporations and state and central governments

The industrial disputes Act defines a collective agreement as one between

a) an employer or employers(which includes a body or trade union of employers)
b) any workmen or trade union or unions consisting of workmen

and which relates to the terms and conditions of employment of any workmen, or to privileges, rights or duties of any employer or employers or any workmen or any trade union or unions consisting of workmen, or to the manner of settlement of any industrial dispute.

What is included in an agreement reached through collective bargaining will depend on the needs and requirements of the parties to the agreement. They could be industry or workplace specific. Despite this, the following would be likely topics covered by the process of collective bargaining:

• Wages, salaries increments and bonus payments

- Hours of work and overtime hours/rates
- Terms and conditions of work, safety, welfare and health care
- Grievance procedures
- Labour productivity, labour standards and modernisation
- Union-management relations including worker participation

The range of the economy and its institutions that the certifications of the unions or associations cover also affects the scope of collective bargaining. Most commonly, these are distinguished as to whether the representation is for an individual plant or employing organisation, an industry comprising a number of employers, or the economic institutions of a nation.

*Plant Level :*

In these negotiations agreements are reached between management of an independent business unit and the union representing the workers of that unit. They are confined to issues at the business unit level and there is no involvement of other unions in other units or industries. This is very common in India.

*Industry Level :*

In this process the unions of many business units form an association and hold discussion with similar associations of owners/managements of such units. Agreements reached are binding on all such units and implemented accordingly. It prevents different terms and conditions being applicable to different units in the same industry or across industries. Sometimes, in certain industries, this level of agreement is negotiated to cover issues of common interest to the units that comprise it but other contracts are negotiated at the plant level to cover issues of varying interest to the individual units.

*National Level :*

The issues common to all workers across industries, regions and even sectors are discussed between representatives of the National Trade Unions and representatives in industry and the business community. Although rare in India, this is very common to the USA where the AFL-CIO enters into national level agreements.

## 9.4.2 The Process of Collective Bargaining

As noted, collective bargaining is governed and informed by a range laws, rules, regulations and protocols. Accordingly, the process encompasses the following major phases:

1. A charter of demands by the bargaining agent
2. Preparation for negotiation
3. Bargaining
4. Collective Agreement
5. Contract administration

A union needs to be registered in order that it may be recognised. A recognised union could become the bargaining agent empowered to hold discussions with management on behalf of the employees in the organisation. If there is more than one union, the union having the majority membership is recognised as the bargaining agent. In some countries, the legislation allows only one bargaining agent for a defined unit of workers. Many employers have several such defined units of workers, differentiated on the basis of criteria such as the trade or skills involved, that are often represented by different unions. In these countries, each unit so defined collectively bargains with the employer for a separate contract. Each union prepares the charter of demands. Where there is an existing agreement the union will usually raise their new demands a few months before the expiry of such agreement.

Both managements and unions prepare themselves for negotiations. Management will prepare by collecting data on employee performance records, labour standards, productivity, absenteeism, accidents, turnover, profit etc. This data is available internally. External data gathered would include economic data, cost of living, copies of similar contracts signed by other unions, terms and conditions of similar employees in other organisations.

Based on data and analysis, management assesses the expectations of similar unions elsewhere and the terms of the agreements that have been agreed to. This will help management decide the percentage increase in wages they ought to consider, balance viability with labour costs, balance the interests of labour with those of the shareholder, and consider constraints on pricing with regard to the competition.

Managements would also consider prioritising the demands, the stand they should take with the union. Similarly, unions collect data and formulate their policies and strategies based on their negotiating power, market conditions, management's capacity to pay and general public support to their cause.

Bargaining usually takes place in a business-like climate. No accusations are made or each other's motives questioned. Their respective positions are presented, supported by facts and figures. Demands may be taken one after the other or on a basis agreed to at the beginning of negotiations. Some demands may be conceded at the beginning. Prerogatives of management may be questioned by the unions with a view to enlarge its scope of influence on management. Managements usually do not allow such encroachment in to areas they consider as being their prerogative. A total rejection of demands would certainly lead to deadlock and is certain to lead to a strike/lock out. Collective bargaining is successful when there is a give and take attitude on both sides, when communication channels are always kept open, when the both sides have the capacity to read the other's true intentions and act 'win-win.'

The terms agreed to have to be reduced to writing. This writing is variously referred to as the collective agreement, labour contract, union contract, or labour–management contract. Companies usually print and circulate them to all relevant parties. The agreement is binding on both parties, has legal status, and serves as a day-to-day guide for labour-management relations. Once the contract has been ratified, its administration follows. Good practice dictates that its administration be transparent: clear with respect to the handling of contractual disputes, and loyal to the spirit of the agreement.

## Collective Bargaining and the Right to Strike

Though precedent setting has made the processes of collective bargaining more and more predictable, collective bargaining does not always have a smooth flow. Many things may happen that prevent both sides from keeping the process from moving. In the USA three things can happen when an impasse develops.
- Conciliation or mediation
- A strike or a lockout
- Arbitration

In India and Sri Lanka, impasses more often lead to strikes than the other two options. However, trends in recent recessionary times have shown a greater willingness on both sides to resort to the other two options.

In some countries, a strike is seen as a refusal to fulfil work obligations at best, but in others only a few categories are outright illegal. The employer aims unfair labour practice strikes at protesting illegal conduct. A 'wildcat strike' is an unauthorised strike occurring during the term of a contract. A 'sympathy strike' occurs when one union strikes in support of the strike of another.

In other jurisdiction, such as India and Sri Lanka, a different taxonomy may be more appropriate:
- Economic strike – This takes place when employee/union demands on wages, working hours and terms and conditions of employment are not met.

- Wildcat strike – This is a quick, sudden and unauthorised stoppage of work and is illegal.
- Sit-down strike – In this type of action, employees get to their places/points of work but refuse to work.
- Sympathy strike – In this, employees or the union is not connected with the dispute, but strike in order to show their solidarity with the striking union. In the USA such a strike is illegal under the Taft-Hartley Act.

## Policies for Collective Bargaining

There are laws and rules governing the establishment of unions and collective agreements. However, laws cannot dictate good union-management relations and the effective administration of jointly negotiated agreements. These outcomes require a commitment and will of intent from both parties. Collective bargaining can be most effective when there is evidence of a number of characteristics in the relationship and on the parts of managements and unions separately.

Collective bargaining must be treated as a form of finding the best solution to a given problem. This calls for a give-and-take attitude from both sides so that both sides gain.

- The parties must have equal power. As with any situation involving the interests of two parties, an inequality in the strengths of such parties can lead to ruthless hegemony, constant conflict and at best a benevolent generosity that the weaker party recognises can easily be taken away.
- There must be mutual trust and confidence. An absence, or perceived absence, of goodwill can lead to acrimony and conflict that make it near impossible to negotiate and maintain mutually satisfying and productive agreements.
- Both negotiating teams should have leadership qualities. During negotiations, it is essential that the parties know that the commitments being proposed by each negotiating team have high probability of acceptance by the parties that the negotiators represent. Their leadership effectiveness in convincing the members is critical.
- The agreement reached must be in conformity with the law of the land. Obviously, the obvious and accepted legality of the agreement is a fundamental requirement. The agreement is a legal document, binding on both parties.

Management, as a party to the agreement, can contribute to lasting harmony by observing a number of practices:

1.  Follow a realistic labour policy that is uniform and consistent across all sections and divisions.
2.  Consider the union a partner not an adversary.
3.  Monitor rules and regulations continuously and bring about changes if such changes improve morale and motivation. Do not take things for granted.
4.  While being careful not to contravene the terms of the agreement, be proactive and address the needs of the workers before it becomes a union-management issue.
5.  Consistently recognise the rights and authority of the bargaining unit.
6.  Give adequate attention to social issues while addressing economic issues.

Equally, the unions have a role to play:
1.  Appreciate the financial constraints of an organisation when presenting demands. Ultimately, the survival of the organisation is more important than gaining all the demands of the employees.
2.  Realise that rights have corresponding duties and not pursue workers' rights alone but discharge duties so that the organisation benefits
3.  Avoid threats and unfair trade practices to coerce managements into granting union demands.
4.  Be democratic and act with total integrity.
5.  Use the strike weapon only as a last resort

So, it is apparent that there is much more to achieving and maintaining strong, productive and effective union-management relations than simply meeting the minimal legal requirements of collective bargaining.

*****

# 10 HUMAN RESOURCE INNOVATION

## 10.1 Introduction

Innovation is at the heart of organizations' success because it allows them to improve the quality of products and services, increase efficiency, cut costs, meet the changing needs of customers, increase sales and profits, gain a greater market share and differentiate themselves from competitors. However, HRM innovation is an understudied area. Lacks of such knowledge, managers often rely on gut feeling, speculation, and their own limited experience about the keys to innovation success. To address this issue, we have to examine organizational innovation through the lens of human resource management (HRM) practices.

One of the challenges facing organizations in the recent economic era is increasing their responsiveness to radical changes in market demands as well as the effective deployment of new technology and ways of working. Innovation of products and internal processes has evidently become a necessity in meeting these demands. However, innovation is no longer solely a task of specialists, scientists or R&D professionals. Nowadays, many practitioners and academics endorse the view that organizations should foster, develop and use the innovative potential of their employees as a means to organizational success. Unleashing the innovative potential within the workforce is believed to be a factor in gaining competitive advantage often reflected in quality management and 'continuous improvement' initiatives. A growing number of academics focus on the determinants of innovation by individuals in organizations.

There is no doubt about the importance of innovation. As markets become increasingly globalised and competitive and the pace of technological change grows, organizations have to compete not only in terms of quality and cost, but also in terms of time-to-market and innovativeness of their products. De Leede and Looise (2005) found that most approaches to innovation and its management in an organizational setting entail an important role for HRM. Further, while there has been a significant amount of attention directed by innovation management scholars to such issues human resource development, rewards, career management and team building, HRM researchers have tended to ignore innovation, particularly at the project level.

Knowledge based theory of the firm is developed in recent contributions in economic and management literature and describe approaches which organize knowledge creation and increased performance of information and communication technologies and the way knowledge can be accessed and disseminated much more readily. Employees, competencies and knowledge constitute a competitive advantage the firm can be presented as a competent team where a tacit organizational competence improves the productivity through selecting and allocating competent people. Therefore HRM practices are important and constitute one of the most strategically relevant resources. Using individuals or systems of HR practices, the strategic HRMP contribute to firm performance.

What drives people to be creative and to improve things in their work? The motivation of employees to engage in proactive or extra-role behaviour is the focus of research on concepts such as 'organizational citizenship behaviour' (OCB, Organ, 1988), 'personal initiative' (Frese Kring, Soose and Zempel, 1996), 'employee creativity' (Oldham & Cummings, 1996) or 'critical reflective behaviour' (van Woerkom, 2003). The notion of employees voluntarily 'doing more than is required' is also present in the concept of innovation. The innovation process not only encompasses the development of creative ideas, but also the implementation of these ideas. The notion of innovative work behaviour (IWB) (Janssen, 2000) takes both aspects into account. IWB concerns the voluntary willingness by individual employees to constitute on-the job innovations – for example, the upgrading of ways of working, communication with direct colleagues, the use of computers, or the development of new services or products.

## 10.1.1 Type of Innovation

There are two type of innovation such as incremental and radical innovation; these radical and incremental describe different types of technological process innovation. Radical innovations are fundamental changes that represent revolutionary changes in technology whereas incremental innovations are minor improvements or simple adjustments in current technology"(Dewar andDutton,1986). The two types of innovation have different antecedents and a different impact on organizational out- comes.

While there is a general consensus that innovation is a 'good thing', there is however little consensus how to define and measure innovation (Rickards, 1996). In research, the focus on innovation on an individual level has tended to be on creativity or suggestion making, rather than on implementation. Both creativity and implementation are components of innovation (Axtell et al., 2000). Innovation work behaviour is conceived as a complex behaviour consisting of four interrelated sets of behavioural activities, namely (1) problem recognition, (2) idea generation, (3) idea promotion and (4) idea realization.

The dimensions of the employee's job and organizational context that are related to individual innovation work behaviour , The design of jobs has long been considered an important contributor to employees' motivation to innovate (Axtell et al., 2000). The Job Characteristics Model (Hackman & Oldham, 1980) is still one of the leading theoretical principles (Parker, Wall & Cordery, 2001) regarding research on job design at an individual level. It identifies the core job characteristics: skill variety, task identity, task significance, autonomy and feedback that affect outcomes such as work satisfaction, job performance and reduced absence and turnover, through so-called 'critical psychological states'. These mediating effects of employee attitudes between the design of a job and relevant employee and work outcomes are originally clustered into three states: experienced meaningfulness of the work, experienced responsibility for the work and knowledge of results of work activities. They mediate the motivating potential of the job with relevant work outcomes for innovation.

## 10.2 Present and Future HRM Innovation

Human resource management (HRM) will be a key area of focus in future as companies and government organizations put in place strategies to cope with the economic crisis and recovery. The so called "war for talent" is on the backburner as the focus shifts to hiring freezes, benefits and compensation cost management, and workforce reductions in the hardest-hit segments. HRM technology solutions can help savvy human resources (HR) professionals strategically manage through the crisis and prepare as the climate shifts to the upside. Trends that we would follow in future include managing and developing talent, embracing HRM analytics, HRMIS, Web3.0 and HR technology strategy.

Employee performance and development will drive business performance. Employee performance objectives will become more aligned with business goals. Firms will attempt to get a grasp on and drive employee skills and competencies through performance management and development to support strategic decisions. In the future HRM will be more challenges and innovative ;

*The workforce is becoming younger and more global;* Despite off shoring and labour arbitrage will continue as companies invest in globalization. Inexperienced new workers will continue to replace retiring baby boomers, encouraging more investment in extended on boarding and talent development programs. The following technology and business process-driven trends will be evident in HRM. Web-based HR will become institutionalized. Social technologies are critical to reaching and connecting with the younger workforce, infusing and retaining knowledge, and turbo-charging programs such as alumni relations and mentoring. Fifty-five percent of HR decision-makers agree that this innovation is very important, but 51% believe that their current tools and process capabilities are below average. This means that HR pros will start to augment their transactional process-based apps by institutionalizing today's rogue social technologies.

*Core HR systems strategies will focus on master data;* The notion of a single source of truth for who works for the company today is still an elusive goal. Based on pioneering work done with customer data hubs, we will start to see strategies evolve for master data management related to the employee life cycle. This will enable the employee data to be kept in sync across multiple HR, payroll, benefits, and talent management systems, as well as third-party business partners and operational applications that use employee data.

*The definition of the workforce will continue to evolve;* Whereas the workforce has traditionally meant employees who are actually on the payroll, business needs encompass tracking and provisioning a variety of "nonemployees" as well. "Nonemployees include contractors, consultants, temporary workers, volunteers, and others who represent part of the productive workforce. Nonemployees will be managed within the human resource management system (HRMS) to allow for headcount and productivity analysis, project staffing, security provisioning, training programs, and other HR-related processes.

*Talent management initiatives and solutions will become more integrated;* The best of- breed application vendors and enterprise resource planning vendors who offer strategic HR capabilities have been touting and educating buyers about the importance of integrated HR technologies. The real benefit of integration is the ability to leverage employee data across historically soloed processes such as recruiting, performance management, succession planning, compensation management, and learning management. Having fewer HR systems and vendors to manage lowers IT support and integration costs and provides a more consistent user experience for business stakeholders.

*Analytics will help HR become more strategic;* Traditional metrics that answer "what was" or "what is" will remain to prove operational return on investment, but they will pale in priority compared to forward-looking analytics. Why? Analytics are the cornerstone to predicting and modeling "what-if " scenarios. They will arm HR with the ability to predict the future results of process and technology changes made today.

*HR outsourcing initiatives will become more focused and selective;* The notion of outsourcing a broad set of HR processes and systems has less and less support. Many of these attempted initiatives have failed to deliver the expected cost savings and service-level goals, and vendors aren't making any money. Outsourcing selective HR processes of a compliance intensive or repetitive nature, like payroll, will remain viable. Cost savings is becoming less of a driver of HR outsourcing, with expertise and reliability being higher priorities.

*HRM will continue to lead in software-as-a-service (SaaS) adoption;* We have to continue to find the SaaS model to be more accepted in HRM than other application areas with the possible exception of customer relationship management. Expect to see continued growth of this deployment model in future. Advancements in software technology related to configurability and integration help to make the SaaS model more palatable to bigger companies, especially those that are weary of upgrading on-premise HRM solutions.

*HR will Be More Business-Focused and Less Dependent On Internal IT;* The traditional HR shop has been heavily focused on managing records in monolithic systems, processing routine transactions, and dealing with compliance and legal issues. This type of HR function has been viewed by top management as a candidate for outsourcing, along with other back-office tasks. The more enlightened HR organization is focused on talent as a strategic resource to make the overall business successful.

HR professionals are acquiring more business acumen as HR processes and talent initiatives are becoming more integrated with the day-to-day operations of the lines of business. On the technology front, HR is becoming less technophobic, more self-sufficient, and less dependent on corporate IT. HRM applications are being designed to be owned and managed by the business stakeholders while also being deployed via a vendor managed, SaaS model. These parallel developments signal the ascendancy of the HR function as a more prominent player in strategic business growth.

## 10.3 The Management of Innovation

We turn to the management of innovation literature for insights concerning delays in implementing novel ideas. As argued in that literature implementing organizational innovations is dependent upon an appreciation of the attributes of a focal innovation (Damanpour, 1991; Wolfe, 1995). Attributes that are most relevant to the adoption and implementation of HRM innovations are as follows:
  • Uncertainty—lack of knowledge concerning the link between an innovation's inputs, processes, and outcomes;
  • Organizational Focus—administrative versus technical—the aspect of the organization to which the innovation is most relevant;
  • Radicalness—the extent to which an innovation is novel, represents change, and thus implies new behaviors;
  • Magnitude—the extent of change to existing structure, personnel, and financial resources implied by an innovation; and
  • Pervasiveness—the number of organizational members who are expected to change their behaviors due to the innovation (Wolfe, 1995).

While uncertainty is inherent to the implementation of most innovations (Storey, 2004), given that they are intangible, administrative innovations, HRM innovations tend to be characterized by considerable uncertainty. Radicands, magnitude, and pervasiveness can each contribute to the uncertainty that surrounds the implementation of an HRM innovation. Uncertainty, in turn, contributes to innovation resistance, which is often unrelated to the objective merit of an innovation, depending rather on the structural and personal consequences it implies. In addition to an innovation's attributes, organizational context is an

PEOPLE MANAGEMENT PRACTICE

important determinant of innovation adoption and implementation (Damanpour, 1991).

In tradition bound organizations, strategic frames of reference, which had provided direction, often become blinders; established processes, which had provided efficiencies, become mindless routines; commitment to particular constituencies (employees, suppliers), which had provided resources, restricts flexibility; and values, which once unified and inspired, harden into rigid rules and regulations (Sull, 1999). Tradition-bound organizations thus are not prone to change, certainly not to radical innovation (Hamel, 1996; Miller, 1990) as "core capabilities" become "core rigidities" (Leonard-Barton, 1992).

Given the uncertainty surrounding most HRM innovations (HRMIs) and due to potential resistance, HRMI implementation is determined by a combination of the power of an innovation champion and by organizational context. The presence of an innovation champion—the individual who provides energy and momentum to the implementation process by advocating and promoting an innovation—is an important determinant of successful innovation implementation (Howell & Higgins, 1990). A champion's efforts are necessary to counter inherent organizational resistance to change; a new idea either finds a champion or dies (Schon, 1976). Predicting HRMI consequences is inherently uncertain, and the innovation's very existence can be threatening to vested interests, so such innovations tend to stimulate political activity (Johns, 1993).

The relative power of organizational actors resolves such activity. While a champion is necessary to personify and make an administrative innovation tangible, his/her power is also necessary to counter threatened groups with necessary power and authority (Galbraith, 1982). A critical component of successful implementation of HRMIs, therefore, is the existence and power of an innovation champion (Wolfe, 1995). In addition to the power of the innovation champion, organizational context is an important determinant of HRMI implementation.

These two innovation determinants—champion power and organizational context—interact in HRMI implementation such that one can compensate for the other (Wolfe, 1995). The more congruent an innovation is with an organization's context, the less "pushing" of the innovation and trying to enlist increasing levels of organizational support is necessary on the part of the champion. Hamel and Getz (2004) argue that to counter such convention and resulting inertia with radical innovation, an understanding must emerge that standard industry practices have become "dogma" justified solely by precedent. An innovation champion, therefore, is necessary to challenge deeply held convention. In addition, a seminal element of organizational context, discontinuities in technology, is often an important determinant of radical innovation (Hamel & Getz, 2004).

According to Barney (1991), a firm's resources "include all assets, capabilities, organizational processes, firm attributes, information, knowledge, etc. Controlled by a firm that enable the firm to conceive of and implement strategies that improve its efficiency and effectiveness". As argued by Barney (1995), the RBV stipulates that firms are endowed with heterogeneous bundles of resources and that competitive advantage accrues if, and only if, a resource (or bundle of resources) is: adopting a saber metrics-type approach to HR should require an energetic and charismatic champion. (1) valuable, in the sense of enabling an organization to conceive of and/or implement strategies that exploit opportunities and/or improve its effectiveness and (2) rare, among current and potential competitors. A resource that is possessed by a large number of organizations will not be a source of competitive advantage.

The recent obsessions with human capital management, HR metrics, and HRIS have tended to travel parallel paths with little synergy. While some of the metrics have focused on human capital, and human capital might be an input to an HRIS, what seemingly has been missing is an integrated approach to human capital strategy that realizes the synergies among these different components. Such as focus on talent (human capital), on statistics (metrics) and recently on information technology, These three levers all now exist within the larger corporate environment, but the question remains concerning who will be the first to integrate them, and thus, identify and exploit the information asymmetries that exist.

The Competencies of HR Professionals will have to change As academics that have taught HR professionals throughout their undergraduate and graduate careers, we have had numerous opportunities to observe how they approach certain courses within the curriculum. Regardless of the university, future HR practitioners almost universally why away from the more analytical classes such as statistics, research methods, operations management, management information systems, accounting, and finance. Now believers of the importance of statistical evaluation are infiltrating management.

## 10.4 E-Commerce and HRM Innovation

The e-commerce approach to people management is popularly believed to be radically new and an innovative rewriting of the 'old' rules of employment. Yet little is known about which HR practices are used by such companies, and what might explain these companies' policy selections in the realm of HR.

Kalakota and Whinston (1997) define e-commerce, or e-business, as 'the buying and selling of information, products and services via computer networks'. Hence, we define an e-commerce firm as one that conducts its trade primarily through a digital infrastructure, including the Internet and related technologies. This definition adapts that of Coltman et al. (2000), with the word 'primarily' replacing their phrase 'in whole, or in part', since the latter covers every organization is making even minor use of the technology.

In the late 1990s few commentators could resist predicting that e-commerce and the Internet would herald a revolution in the world of work (Leadbetter, 1999; Venkatraman, 2000). One such transformation was to come from the widespread adoption of the apparently 'radical' e-commerce approach to organizational design, operating principles and structures, and people management (Hoogervorst et al., 2002). E-commerce firms were lauded for their 'practices that support autonomy, collaboration and innovation' (Boudreau et al., 2000: 3), namely flatter organizational structures, 'fluid and impermanent project-based' job designs, more informal and more inclusive decision-making, and reward schemes combining individualized and collective incentives. Yet beyond stereotypical images of 'heroic teams of self-directed workers . . . non-hierarchical surroundings . . . the vague promise of bounteous rewards from stock options and a culture of overwork and burnout' and spectacular tales of managerial excess, little is known about the actual human resource (HR) strategies and practices inside such firms.

In the great majority of the books and articles on e-commerce, neither HR nor 'employee management' in general is even of peripheral interest Isabel E.V et.al (2008). The specific literature emphasizes instead technological concerns, marketing strategies, networking and the process of securing financial backing. Indeed, the literature tends 'to portray organization-building as at best irrelevant or at worst a source of organisational drag in a world operating at "Internet speed"' (Baron and Hannan, 2002: 8). Wright and Dyer (2001: 24) note, however, that, while commentary in the business press rarely suggests as much, many failures among entrepreneurial e-commerce firms 'clearly come from the inability to deal with organizational and people challenges – rather than lack of vision, great technology or even business savvy'.

Evidence of the marginalization of HR issues comes from two studies. Feindt et al. (2002) acknowledged 'attention to good employee relations' as one of 'six common factors associated with successful growth companies', but then declined to investigate this variable further in their research. They offered no explanation for its omission, almost as though it were self-explanatory? Similarly, Finkelstein (2001) called for research into the 'mistakes' made by failed ecommerce start-ups along four dimensions of business strategy – customers, capabilities, competitive advantage and internal consistency. Though each has clear implications for managing employees, he neglected the lessons that might be learned from examining firms' 'mistakes' in HR and organizational design.

Among the few to conduct empirical research into HR-related matters inside e-commerce firms Horner-Long and Schoenberg (2002) compared the value attached to certain leadership attributes in a sample split evenly between ecommerce firms and 'traditional' companies. They found commonalities, but the 'e-leaders' valued risk-taking, networking, project management and technical knowledge more than their traditional counterparts, and seemed less concerned with honesty and collaboration.

Kanter (2001) drew on findings from her 'Global E-Culture Survey' identify four key strategic and organizational implications of e-commerce: treating strategy formulation as 'improvisational theatre' (in essence, encouraging innovation), nurturing networks of partners, turning organizations into 'communities' and creating a culture that attracts and retains the best talent.

### 10.4.1 e-HRM Innovation:

e-HRM is a way of implementing HR strategies, policies, and practices in organizations through a conscious and directed support of and/or with the full use of web-technology-based channels. The word 'implementing' in this context has a broad meaning, such as making something work, putting something into practice, or having something realized. E-HRM, therefore, is a concept - a way of 'doing' HRM.

e-HRM guided by the research to develop a model for e-HRM inspired by the thoughts and ideas expressed. The steps towards the model, when combined, form a chain of reasoning: the basis for the model. The steps, or parts of the model, will be:

1. The state of HRM in an organization.
2. The e-HRM goals.
3. Types of e-HRM.
4. HRM outcomes.

The state of HRM in an organization:

Organizations do not start with nothing when they step out onto the e-HRM road. For a start there will be certain implicit or explicit HRM policy assumptions and practices already in use. Further, every management decision contains some HRM component. The set of HRM policy choices within an organization can be categorized into one of the three types distinguished by Beer et al.: the bureaucratic policy, the market policy, and the clan policy. From the existing state of the HRM in an organization, the individuals and groups involved make choices with regard to e-HRM. As these are made within a certain context, the choices are purpose-driven.

e-HRM goals:

What goals drive stakeholders when deciding about e-HRM? Based upon a scan of professionally oriented and academic journals, we can draw conclusions about the reasons or goals of organizations making steps towards e-HRM. The four 'pressures' from Lepak and Snell (1998) are a good start, but we think that they can be reduced to three types of goals, namely:

1. Improving the strategic orientation of HRM
2. Cost reduction/efficiency gains
3. Client service improvement/facilitating management and employees.

Types of e-HRM:

E-HRM is not a specific stage in the development of HRM, but a choice for an approach to HRM. Wright and Dyer (2000) distinguish three areas of HRM where organizations can choose to 'offer' HR services face-to-face or through an electronic means: transactional HRM, traditional HRM, and transformational HRM. Lepak and Snell (1998) make a similar distinction, namely operational HRM, relational HRM and transformational HRM.

e-HRM outcomes:

We assume, based upon Beer et al.'s ideas about the expected results or an outcome of HRM, that e-HRM also aims to achieve a certain set of outcomes. All HRM activities, and therefore also all e-HRM activities, will implicitly or explicitly be directed towards these 'overall' outcomes. Beer et al. (1984) distinguish four possibilities: high commitment, high competence, cost effectiveness, and higher congruence. These outcomes, in turn, may change the state of HRM in an organization, or through individuals and/or groups within an organization actually result in a new HRM state.

Less administrative tasks for the HR department and therefore less administrative positions, more focus on the strategic goals of the organization and therefore an HRM staff consisting mainly of 'thinkers'; this is, in essence, what HR departments can expect or are already facing and experiencing. From our definition of, and approach to, e-HRM the following can be concluded about the consequences of e-HRM for the HR department. E-HRM will assume an active role for line management and employees in implementing HRM strategies, policies, and practices. In terms of the more operational and information processing work, such as administration, registration and information distribution, there will be less demand for HR people. This seems most logical for organizations with an operational e-HRM approach. However, also with a relational e-HRM approach dominating, a smaller HR staff will be necessary if line management and employees.

## 10.5 HR Fit for Innovation

In the current high-tech environment, enabling technological innovation is essential to firms' survival. However, it is difficult for firms to acquire by themselves all the required technological capabilities in a short period of time. Hence, the formation of technological strategic alliances is becoming increasingly an important tool to face the innovation challenge. The alliance potential for innovation increases as the amount of complementary technological knowledge does (Lane and Lubatkin, 1998), thus, technological multi-partner alliances (MAs) are gaining more and more popularity (Lavie et al., 2007). The complex functioning of this kind of collaboration usually relies on the creation of multiple temporary project teams. These teams are composed of members from different partners and are in charge of attaining innovation. Henceforth, we will refer to them as multi-partner-alliance teams. Understanding innovation dynamics in multi-partner alliances teams may have important implications for research and for alliance and team management. However, despite the extensive existing literature on innovation teams, there is still a lack of research about the issue. This paper aims to fill this literature gap, by focusing on the impact of HRM fit from a holistic perspective.

Teams represent one of the organizational structures with greatest potential for innovation. However, the creation of multiple multi-partner alliances teams in a technological alliance does not guarantee the collaboration success. To make this possible, a proper climate supporting learning, creativity and innovation need to be generated for each of the multi-partner alliances teams of the alliance (Argote et al. 2001, Paulus et al., 2001). In attaining that, human resources management (HRM) may play a key role. Thus, if the firm systematically fosters HRM fit by adopting an appropriate system of HRM practices, competitive advantages may be achieved, including those from innovation (Laursen and Foss, 2003). Traditionally, two dimensions of HRM fit have been established: vertical fit (alignment between HRM practices and firm's strategic goals) and horizontal fit (HRM practices mutually complementary).

With regard to HRM fit effects, multi-partner alliances teams and any other type of innovation team could have something in common, but there are some peculiarities which They are composed of individuals from different partners, which have different strategic patterns, in particular, different HRM styles. In order to provide better understanding about the innovation dynamics in multi-partner alliances teams, it is necessary to go beyond the traditional dimensions of HRM fit. Isabel E.V et.al (2008) propose a new multi-level conceptualization for HRM fit to be relevant for multi-partner alliances teams, by including a new dimension ('relational HRM fit'). This new dimension allows to create internal consistency within each multi-partner alliances team when exists.

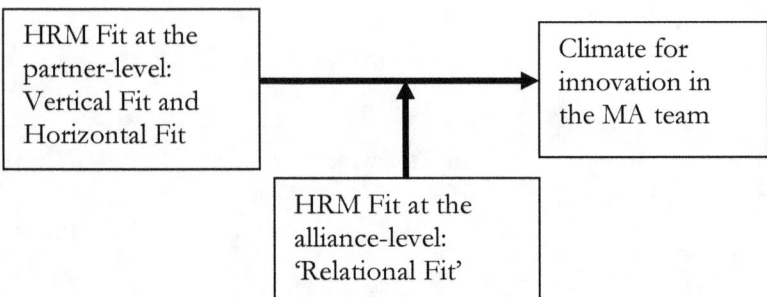

Figure 1.Multi-level HRM fit for innovation in multi-partner alliances MA teams by Isabel E.V et.al (2008)

HRM has been well-established as a key factor in promoting organizational learning and innovation, as well as in managing innovation teams. Thus, the design of HRM practices may also play a key role in generating a proper team climate for innovation. More specifically, the strategic approach of HRM traditionally has established two main dimensions of HRM fit: vertical fit and horizontal fit. Scholars have expanded the issue of HRM fit by considering other dimensions, like organizational or institutional fit or person-environment fit.

Little is known yet about the contribution of HRM fit to the functioning of innovation teams. However, it has been addressed theoretically and empirically the link between HRM fit and firm's innovativeness. HRM fit may contribute to generate such climate in any type of innovation teams. Nevertheless, the unique characteristics of multi-partner alliances teams drive the necessity of reconceptualising the notion of HRM fit.

*****

REFERENCES:

Armstrong, M (1999). A Handbook of Personnel Practice, 6th ed., London: Kogan Page.

Armstrong, M (2000). "The name has changed but has the game remained the same?" Employee Relations, Vol. 22 No. 6, pp. 576-593.

Arm strong Michael, (2 0 0 1 ) A Handbook of Human Resource Management, Eighth edition, London: Kogan Paul.

Armstrong, M. (2009) A Handbook of Human Resource Management Practice, London: Kogan Page

Axtell et al. (2000) Axtell, C.M., Holman, D.J., Unsworth, K., Wall, T.D., Waterson, P.E. & Harrington, E. Shopfloor innovation: Facilitating the suggestion and implementation of ideas. Journal of Occupational and Organizational Psychology, 2000, 73, 265–85.

Barney (1991): Firm Resources and Sustained competitive Advantage, Journal of Management, Vol.17,No.1,99-120.

Baron and Hannan, (2002). Baron, James N. and Michael T. Hannan. 2002. "Organizational blueprints for success in high-tech start-ups: Lessons from the Stanford Project on Emerging Companies." California Management Review 44 : 8–36.

Bartlett and Ghoshal, (1991) Managing Across Borders: the transnational solution, Boston, Massachusetts: Harvard Business School Press.

Bateman and Snell (1999) Bateman, Thomas S. and Scott A. Snell. (1999). Management: Building a Competitive Advantage, 4th ed., Boston: Irwin/McGraw-Hill.

Beardwell Ian and Len Holden (2 0 0 1 ) Human Resource Management: a contemporary approach, Third edition, Harlow England: FT Prentice Hall

Beardwell, I. and L. Holden (1999) Human Resource Management: A Contemporary Perspective, London: Pitman

Michael Beer, Bert Spector, Paul R. Lawrence, D. Quinn Mills, and Richard E. Walton,(1984): Managing Human Assets, , New York: The Free Press,

Bell, A. (2000) Transforming Your Workplace, London: Institute of Personnel and Development

Bittel & Newstrom, (1990). What Every Supervisor should know, Westerville, OH: Glencoe/Mcgraw-Hill.

Boudreau et al., (2000)' Human Resource Metrics: Can Measures be Strategic,' Research in Personnel and Human Resources Management, Supplement 4, 75-98

Boxall, P. F. Spring (1992). Strategic human resource management: beginnings of a new theoretical sophistication. Human Resource Management Journal. 2(3).

Civi, E (2000). "Knowledge management as a competitive asset: a review", Marketing Intelligence & Planning, Vol. 18 No. 4, pp. 166-174.

Cooper and Payne, (2000) The people's republic opens its doors to people management, People Management,26 October, pp16–17

Crainer, S. (2000) The Management Century: A Critical Review of Twentieth Century Thought and Practice, London:John Wiley

Dalton, P. and G. Dunnett (1992) A Psychology for Living: Personal Construct Psychology for Professional Clients,Chichester: John Wiley & Sons

Damanpour, et al.(1998),"Successful knowledge management projects", Sloan Management Review, Vol. 39 No. 2, pp. 43-57.

Farnham, D. (2000) Employee Relations in Context, London: CIPD

Filius, R, de Jong, J A and Roelofs, E C (2000), "Knowledge Management in the HRD office: a comparison of three cases", Journal of Workplace Learning, Vol. 12 No. 7, pp. 286-295.

Galbraith, (1982) Strategy implementation: the role of structure and process. St. Paul: West.

Gary Dessler, ( 2008) Human Resource Management, 11th Edition, Prentice Hall, Inc.

Glueck, W. F. (1982). Personnel: a diagnostic approach. Revised by Milkovich. 3rd ed. Dallas, Texas: Business Publications Inc.

Graham, H.T. and R. Bennett (1999) Human Resources Management, London: Financial Times/Pitman

Gratton, L. (2000) Living Strategy: Getting People at the Heart of Corporate Purpose, London: Financial Times/Prentice Hall

Halman, D., K. Pavlica and R. Thorpe (1996) Rethinking Kolb's theory of experiential learning: the contribution of social construction and activity theory in Management Learning, 4(24): 485–504

Institute of Personnel and Development (IPD) (2000) Success through learning: the argument for strengthening workplace learning, insert in People Management, 8 June

Isabel E.V et.al (2008) Innovation dynamics in multipatner alliance teams: a focus on human resource management fit, Dpto. de Organización de Empresas y C.I.M.

Ivancevich, J.M. (1998). Human resource management 7th ed. Boston: Irwin McGraw-Hill.

Jackson, T. (2000). Handling grievances. London Chartered Institute of Personnel and Development.

Kandel, E. Lazear, E. (1992) 'Peer Pressure and Partnerships,' Journal of Political Economy, 100:4, 801-17.

Lane, P. J. and Lubatkin, M. (1998): "Relative absorptive capacity and interorganizational learning." Strategic Management Journal 19: 5, pp.

461-477.

Laursen, K. and Foss, N. J. (2003): "New human resource management practices, complementarities and the impact on innovation performance." Cambridge Journal of Economics 27: 2, pp. 243-263.

Laursen, K. and Mahnke, V. (2001): "Knowledge strategies, firm types, and complementarities in human-resource practices", Journal of Management and Governance, 5:1, pp. 1-27.

Lavie, D., Lechner, C. and Singh, H. (2007): "The performance implications of timing of entry and involvement in multipartner alliances." Academy of Management Journal 50: 3, pp. 578-604.

Legge, K. (1995) Human Resource Management: Rhetorics and Realities, Basingstoke: Macmillan – now Palgrave

Linda Maund, (2001). Introduction to Human Resource Management, Palgrave Introduction to human resource management

Mintzberg, H (1989). Mintzberg on Management: Inside Our Strange World of Organisations, NY: Free Press, New York.

Nair, N.G., & Nair, L. 1999. Personnel management and industrial relations. New Delhi: S. Chand & Co. Ltd.

O'Reilly, C. and J. Pfeffer (2000) Hidden Value, Boston: Harvard Business School

Opatha (2000), Human Resource Management: a hand book, University of Sri Jeyawardenapura, Sri Lanka.

Paulus, P. B., Larey, T. S. and Dzindolet, M. T. (2001): Creativity in groups and teams. Groups at work: Theory and Research. M. E. Turner. London, L. Erlbaum Associates.

Pelletier, (2001) Pelletier, K. R. 2001. A review and analysis of the clinical- and cost-effectiveness studies of comprehensive health promotion and disease management programs at the worksite: 1998- 2000 update. American Journal of Health Promotion, 162, 107-116.

Porter, M. E. 1996. "What is a strategy?" Harvard Business Review (November- December), pp. 61-78.

Quinn, J B (1992). Intelligent Enterprise: A Knowledge and Service Based paradigm for Industry, NY: The Free Press, New York.

Robertson, M and Hammersley, G M (2000). "Knowledge management practices within a knowledge-intensive firm: the significance of the people management dimension", Journal of European Industrial Training, Vol. 24 No. 2/3/4, pp. 241-253.

Rothwell, S. (1995) Human Resource Planning in Storey, J. (ed.) Human Resource Management: A Critical Text, London: Routledge

Salamon, M. 1998. Industrial relations theory and practice. 3rd ed. London: Prentice Hall.

Sisson, K. and J. Storey (2000) The Realities of Human Resource Management: Managing the Employment Relationship, Milton

Keynes: Open University Press

Soliman, F and Spooner, K (2000). "Strategies for implementing knowledge management: role of human resources management", Journal of Knowledge Management, Vol. 4 No. 4, pp. 337-345.

Storey, J. (1992) Developments in the Management of Human Resources, Oxford: Blackwell

Suter, E. (2000) The Employment Law Checklist, London: Institute of Personnel and Development

Venkatraman, N. (1989): "The concept of 'Fit' in strategic research: Toward verbal and statistical correspondence". Academy of Management Review, 14(3), pp. 423-444.

Warren, L (1999). "Knowledge management: just another office in the executive suite?", Accountancy Ireland, December.

# ABOUT THE AUTHOR

Vasthiyampillai Sivalogathasan is working as a Senior Lecturer in Management Studies, The Open University Sri Lanka. Sivalogathasan has a B.Com (Hons) Degree from the University of Peradeniya with second class upper division and during the university he won most meritorial prize throughout the years and also at convocation in 1997. He have been awarded postgraduate scholarship for Master of Business Administration by the Asian Institute of Technology, Thailand in 2001. Presently, He has been awarded full Chinese Government Scholarship for Ph.D study in Innovation Management at the Zhejiang University in China.

He has worked as Assistant Lecturer at the University of Peradeniya, as a Assistant Registar at the Vavuniya Campus of the University of Jaffna, as a Human Resource Manager for the INGOs such as Oxfam and Action Against Hunger. He has more than 12 years experience on both government and non-government sectors in multidiscipline aspects.

He has been edited and published three books, many research papers which were published at International and national research publications and many more articles in newspapers and magazines. Also He was awarded several awards and scholarships for undergraduate study as well.

www.ingramcontent.com/pod-product-compliance
Lightning Source LLC
Chambersburg PA
CBHW051513170526
45165CB00002B/461